Our great need is to recover an ~~~~~~~~~~~ of God. In a fresh and engaging ~~~~~~~~ a useful discipleship book for all ⌣~~~~ ant doctrine without frightening jargon and slogans. I look forward to getting it into people's hands and appropriating some wonderful illustrations!

Paul Rees
Lead Pastor, Charlotte Chapel, Edinburgh, Scotland

Lay this to heart: the *most important* thing about you is what you believe about God – because what you know and believe about God will determine how you live out your life. Theology proper, then, is of immense practicality. And here, Orlando Saer's *Big God* is of cosmic practicality as he peels off the cultural shrink- wrap from this massive doctrine and thus gives wings to Christian living – and mission. Here is medicine for the soul!

R. Kent Hughes
Senior Pastor Emeritus, College Church, Wheaton, Illinois

Life is good, and so is God. Do you doubt that? In this little book, hard questions are tackled head on and answered with straight-forward biblical wisdom. If God has seemed absent, He might start appearing for you in surprising places if you take on board Saer's words here. Accurate, biblical, clear, short, serious and practical, in this book thinking meets life. Orlando's illustrations are good, his conclusions useful. The book, among a thousand other things, is a compelling invitation to prayer! Doubt me on any of this? Take it up, read it, and find out for yourself. You won't be sorry you did.

Mark Dever
Pastor, Capitol Hill Baptist Church and President, 9Marks.org, Washington, DC

I love this book by Orlando Saer because God is glorified as the all-powerful, all-knowing, loving and sovereign God! It is theologically rigorous, Biblically compelling, immensely pastoral and hugely practical. Saer unravels all the key questions about God's sovereignty (suffering, evangelism, guidance and prayer) in a fresh and realistic manner, leaving us marvelling at just how big our God really is and the joy of trusting Him at all times. I'd recommend this book to believers so their daily walk with Jesus is enriched through a biblical understanding of God's sovereignty. I'd give this book to the unbeliever to remove the stumbling blocks so often raised about God's sovereignty and human free will. And I'd commend it to pastors for their personal refreshment and for pastoral ministry. Read it, believe it, learn it and live it – you'll find it challenging, comforting, compelling and liberating. Such an important topic and such a good book!

Paul Dale
Senior Pastor, Church by the Bridge, Sydney, Australia

God's sovereign rule and our responsible choices have always been tricky to understand but crucial for everyday Christian living. The danger we face is shrinking God and as a result shrinking our Christian discipleship. With care and balance Orlando Saer unpacks these areas showing us how a bigger God changes living for him. Read and discover how big God really is.

Graham Beynon
Minister, Grace Church, Cambridge

Orlando Saer has seamlessly woven biblical truth into our everyday world of Seinfeld re-runs, Saturday afternoon visits to the art gallery and the weekday commute in this wonderful little book. Though clearly intended for Christian beginners, trust me when I say *Big God* is good therapy for veteran believers like me as well. If your 'god' has been down-sized in the face of issues like election, evangelism, personal guidance and prayer, *Big God* will scale Him back up to size as the Sovereign God of the Universe. This book is fresh, theologically acute and full of pastoral insight: I highly recommend it.

Phil Campbell
Senior Minister, Mitchelton Presbyterian Church, Brisbane, Australia

BIG GOD

How to approach SUFFERING,
spread the GOSPEL,
make DECISIONS and PRAY
IN THE LIGHT OF A GOD WHO REALLY IS IN
the DRIVING SEAT OF THE WORLD

ORLANDO SAER

CHRISTIAN
FOCUS

Unless otherwise indicated, all Scripture quotations are from *The Holy Bible, English Standard Version*, copyright © 2001 by Crossway Bibles, a division of Good News Publishers. Used by permission. All rights reserved. ESV Text Edition: 2007.

Scripture quotations marked (NIV) are taken from *The Holy Bible, New International Version*®, NIV® Copyright © 1973, 1978, 1984, 2011 by Biblica, Inc.™ Used by permission. All rights reserved worldwide.

Scripture quotations marked (NIV 1984) are taken from *The Holy Bible, New International Version*®. NIV®. Copyright©1973, 1978, 1984 by International Bible Society. Used by permission of Zondervan. All rights reserved.

Scripture quotations marked (NASB) are taken from the *New American Standard Bible*®, Copyright © 1960, 1962, 1963, 1968, 1971, 1972, 1973, 1975, 1977, 1995 by The Lockman Foundation Used by Permission. (www.Lockman.org)

Orlando Saer is Senior Pastor of Christ Church Southampton, where he is involved in training and discipling university students. He has previously served churches in Sydney, London and Surrey and is the author of *Iron Sharpens Iron*, a manual for leading Bible-oriented small groups. Formerly a teacher, he is married to Libby and they have four children.

Copyright © Orlando Saer 2014

paperback ISBN 978-1-78191-294-2
epub ISBN 978-1-78191-336-9
mobi ISBN 978-1-78191-337-6

Published in 2014
reprinted 2015
by
Christian Focus Publications Ltd,
Geanies House, Fearn, Ross-shire,
IV20 1TW, Scotland, United Kingdom.
www.christianfocus.com

Cover design by Daniel van Straaten

Printed by Bell and Bain, Glasgow

MIX
Paper from
responsible sources
FSC® C007785

CONTENTS

For my children – Toby, Charis, Barnaby and Nathaniel.
May you always know the joy of serving Him who
'works out everything in conformity with the purpose of His will'

INTRODUCTION

What noises does your mind hear when life goes quiet?

You probably know the experience of your ears retuning at the end of the day. Work is finished, your friends have gone, the TV's off, the people you live with – if you do live with anyone – are fast asleep, the world is quiet. It's then, and perhaps only then, that you notice the sounds from further away. The softer sounds. The wind in the trees, the barking of a dog, the water in the pipes, a distant siren maybe. Perhaps more disturbingly, the creaks, the scratching, the soft bang.

When the world around us goes quiet, those softer sounds – drowned out during the day – come to the fore.

It's just the same for our 'inner ear'.

In the whirl of life for many of us, our minds rarely have time to think. Our jobs, courses, families, friends, social life, leisure activities – not to mention our church programmes – demand all our attention.

But there are quieter moments – from time to time. And when they come, that's when our minds return to those softer, but irritatingly persistent, noises. The nagging questions and doubts about our Christian faith. The conundrums that never get solved.

What do you do with them? If you're like most people, you probably just put them out of your mind. Throw them in the 'too hard' pile. Resolve to set aside some time to ponder them – next year. The one thing you probably *don't* do is sit down and really try to think them through. You've tried that before and it wasn't pretty. You found yourself questioning the most basic faith convictions. Better just to get on with life and block your ears. That's your survival technique.

It's an understandable response. But it's a lazy one – and a dangerous one too.

Lazy, because God has given us minds and expects us to use them to fuel our Christian growth. '...be transformed by the renewing of your mind', writes the apostle Paul in Romans 12:2.

And dangerous, because if we don't work through our issues deliberately, Bible in hand, we'll find that – almost by osmosis – we'll imbibe worldly ways of thinking which will join the dots for us in unbiblical ways. Our thinking will become a patchwork of snippets we've picked up from films, friends, speakers and the Scriptures. Yes, the Bible will be in there. But only as one of a number of influences. Remember why Paul spoke as he did? He deliberately set himself apart from the world 'so that your faith might not rest on men's wisdom, but on God's power' (1 Cor. 2:5, NIV 1984).

This book deals with just one particular set of questions that have perplexed Christian believers. But the trouble they've caused is disproportionate. In my experience as a pastor, they've caused anxiety and confusion among almost all Christian believers at some point. In fact, for many, the joy of the Christian life has been all but extinguished by an ongoing struggle with these issues.

They're all to do with the way God works in the world, and particularly the way his work co-exists with ours.

I've called the book 'Big God', because if you boil the issues down, you could sum up every one of them with a question beginning: 'If God really is so big...?'

- If God really is so big and powerful, why is there so much pain in the world? Surely he'd stop it if he could – but things seem to be going from bad to worse!

- If God really is so big and all-deciding, what does that do to evangelism? When someone comes to Christ is it their own decision or God's – and where does that leave our role in telling others the gospel?

- If God really is so big and authoritative, how does that affect my decision-making? Where should I look to make sure my life stays within his will?

- If God really is so big and in control, where does prayer fit in? What's the *point* of praying if he's got everything planned out – and why don't I always see obvious answers when I do?

If you look down the contents page, you'll see the last four chapters address each of those questions in turn.

But here's a tip. However burning one of those questions is for you right now, don't skip the first two chapters. Really, don't. You're going to have to trust me on this one.

You need to think about how the Bible talks about God's work in the world generally, before you approach any of those specific questions. Otherwise, you just won't 'get' it!

If you're like most people, your instinctive response to these questions will be – perhaps *has* been to date – to shrink God down, and therefore lessen the 'problem'. But redefining God is a fairly drastic thing to do. Drastic and – as I hope you'll see – unnecessary.

I hope this book is a help to you. Whether the questions it addresses are of more academic interest to you, or they really are ongoing, anxiety-inducing, joy-robbing, faith-damaging arrows in your soul, I pray that – as we look at the Bible – the god of our imaginations would be unshrunk until he reaches the full stature of the Big God who is there.

The Curious Case
of the Shrinking God

'The ice is melting!' That was the *Inconvenient Truth* – or at least one part of it – which Al Gore announced to the world back in 2006. His documentary helped to catapult environmental issues from the sidelines on to centre-stage in the theatre of public awareness.

The other part of that 'Inconvenient Truth' – namely, that the melting is down to human activities – remains controversial. The believers seem to have the upper hand at present but the sceptics aren't bowing out just yet. The fight goes on.

However much we're to blame, though, one thing's for sure: the polar caps really are melting away. And they have been, bit by bit, for many years. The satellite pictures tell the story. They've been snapping away for more than twenty years. And every year there's less to see of them.

And it matters. Governments the world over are taking drastic steps to reduce carbon emissions. But at the same time they're spending great time and effort working out the possible effects. What will happen if sea levels rise as they're expected to? How will human life in this or that area be affected? They may not have all the answers but what is clear is that shrivelling ice shelves up at the top of the globe will certainly have knock-on effects for us human beings who live somewhere in the middle of it.

But the polar caps aren't the only things that are shrinking. It turns out the same thing is happening to God. At least, the 'God' that we Christians picture in our hearts and minds. The 'God' that we allow to shape our thoughts, attitudes and decisions. The 'God', in fact, who is preached about in churches, written about in Christian books and presented in seminaries and theological colleges. There's no doubt about it: *that* God is getting smaller – and has been for a long time.

What I want to do in this chapter is to chart the progress of the shrinkage. As I do, I'd like to challenge you to ponder just how diminished *your* God has become.

THE GOD OF THE BIBLE

Awesome. Now there's a word which has lost its edge in recent times. For many, it means... well, nothing really. It's no more than an enthusiastic and affirming way of moving a conversation forward. 'What are you doing this afternoon?' 'I'm going shopping.' 'Awesome. Can you get me some chocolate?'

But the God of the Bible really is 'awesome'. That is, he inspires awe – a sense of open-mouthed wonder, or even hide-behind-a-rock fear – in those who contemplate him. Why? Simple. It's because of how great he is. How wonderfully majestic and dominant he is. Just looking around at the world he made should be enough to establish that: 'Worthy are you, our Lord and God, to receive glory and honour and power, for you created all things and by your will they existed and were created' (Rev. 4:11).

What's more, there are no chinks in his armour. There is no Achilles' heel, no blind-spots. Everything about God is perfectly and consistently good. He's not like the Olympic decathlete who dreads one event – the pole vault perhaps – but hopes that a below-par performance in that department will be more than made up for when it comes to the high jump and the 1500 metres. God is pure quality across the board.

And many of those 'quality' features of his are seen very obviously and naturally in the way he relates to the world. His love, for example. God isn't just 'loving' in theory; no, he *shows* that love in practice. His love for the whole created order leads him to design and put into effect a dramatic and costly plan to smash apart the barrier of sin through the sacrificial work of Christ and bring people into perfect relationship with himself.

And his justice, too. God isn't simply 'just' in a private sense. No, his justice is something that affects the way he deals with human beings. It outs itself in the way he holds human beings to account for the way they live their lives. We can't get away with outrageous, God-defying behaviour. There will be a day of reckoning when our every thought, word and decision will be produced as exhibits in the divine courtroom.

And then of course there's his power. God doesn't keep his power to himself. He applies it to the world. He exercises utter, hands-on, control over every event that happens, without exception. And 'without exception' means exactly that. Nothing is too small to be attributed to God: 'Are not two sparrows sold for a penny? And not one of them will fall to the ground apart from your Father' (Matt. 10:29). At the other end of the scale, nothing and nobody is too big to lie outside his control: nations, kings, even the weather – we learn in the Bible that these are all directed by God.

There are no limits in geography or history to God's control. A quick skim-read of Job 38–39 makes that much clear. There we find God comparing human beings to himself through a series of questions that put Job in his place.

> 'Where were *you* when I laid the earth's foundation? Tell me, if you understand. Who marked off its dimensions?
>
> Who shut up the sea behind doors when it burst forth from the womb?
>
> Have *you* ever given orders to the morning, or shown the dawn its place?
>
> Have *you* journeyed to the springs of the sea or walked in the recesses of the deep?
>
> Have *you* comprehended the vast expanses of the earth?
>
> Do *you* send the lightning bolts on their way? Do they report to you, 'Here we are'?
>
> Do *you* know when the mountain goats give birth?
>
> Will the wild ox consent to serve *you*?
>
> Do *you* give the horse its strength?
>
> Does the hawk take flight by *your* wisdom?
>
> Does the eagle soar at *your* command?'
> (Job 38:4, 8, 12, 16, 18, 35; 39:1, 9, 19, 26-27, NIV)

You get the drift. There's nothing which lies outside the zone of God's control. He stands behind painful things as well as happy ones: 'I bring prosperity and create disaster' (Isa. 45:7, NIV 1984). God is as intentional about the course of an individual human being's life as he is about the course of history as a whole: 'The king's heart is a stream of water in the hands of the Lord; he turns it wherever he will' (Prov. 21:1).

This is the God we're introduced to in the Bible. He's a big God. And he's a God who's in the driving seat, with his hands firmly on the controls.

It may be that in your better moments – when you're on your knees, perhaps, in prayer before your almighty Father God – that this is truly the God you conceive of. The very fact that you're praying gives the game away: you really do believe at that moment that God has it in his power to act. And the particular things you're praying for show just how wide-ranging you believe his power to be.

But barely have you opened your eyes again and stepped back from his throne, then – if you're like many of us – your God has started to shrink.

THE INTERVENING GOD

I love the cruise-control button. It makes driving so much less of a chore, so much less tiring, and so much more pleasurable. Gone is the need to keep switching focus between the speedometer and the road. There's no more fear that a heavy foot and an absent mind might lead to a red face when a speed camera pops up on the horizon. And the great thing is that my right foot is always there, hovering just over the pedal. It's ready to step in when trouble's brewing ahead. How often I do need to take back control will vary depending on the trip. But any obstacle I meet, or any junction I need to negotiate, is no problem. In a split second, I can be fully in charge of the car once more.

Can you see where I'm heading here? Many of us could sign up without any hesitation to the description of the God of the Bible that I gave earlier, at least in theory. But if we're honest, there's often a gap between life and lip. We don't always think or talk – or indeed act – in a way that's consistent with what we say we believe. In practice, we shrink him down to a more manageable size – about the size in fact, of a cruise-control driver. That is, we think of him as quite *capable* of intervening in our lives and affairs (of that we have no doubt), but only occasionally actually doing so. Most of the time he lets things take their course. Just here and there he needs to get somebody out of a scrape, or engineer some meeting, or orchestrate some kind of resolution.

One way to spot if you're a God-shrinker is just to listen to yourself talk. Do you sometimes use the word 'providential'? 'That was so providential, bumping into Joe just when I'd lost my wallet. How else would I have got money for the bus home?' Or what about the language of 'God-things'? 'That was a real God-thing, Joe just happening to appear out of nowhere like that!'

Using expressions like 'providential' or 'God-things' as Christian-speak for 'lucky' is not necessarily a bad thing. Nor is talking about apparent coincidences as 'God-things'. Speaking like that can actually be a helpful way of training ourselves and those around us to see God at work in everyday life.

But there are problems too. One is that different timescales might cause us to think again. Would we still describe the event that way if things had turned out badly? Imagine the bus crashed, and you ended up in hospital. Would you have been so quick to call the meeting 'providential'? Or say Joe started making unwelcome advances towards you over the next few weeks, which he felt he was entitled to after helping you out that day, would you – with hindsight – have described the meeting as a 'God-thing'?

The other problem with talking this way is that we're in danger of training ourselves to see God's work in the world as confined to certain events: perhaps ones which lead to short-term happiness or comfort, or ones which are just extraordinary coincidences. It actually makes our God smaller. It suggests that although he is indeed in the driving seat, he's that 'cruise-control driver': by and large he lets things just take their course, just stepping in from time to time. We might not put it that way if challenged, but in reality that's the way we think about him.

The God of our hearts has started to shrink. Though not as much as he's about to.

THE PAIN-FREE GOD

Wouldn't it be great to have lived in the garden of Eden? At least Eden before serpents, curses and exiles entered the plot? It was a place of beautiful things, of abundant food and of perfect harmony: human beings were able to connect properly with each other, with the natural world and with God. In other words it was a place of perfect happiness and fulfilment. Who wouldn't want to live there?

If that's the kind of life God mapped out for human beings, it's got to say something about where pain fits in, hasn't it? The kind of low-level troubles that all of us experience from day to day – as well as the horrific suffering that make life almost unbearable for some – simply could not come from God. At least that's the way we reason.

I mean, how could they? We know what God's ideal world looked like and suffering wasn't even part of the landscape. When life gets hard for us, it's got to be down to someone else, or something else. It can't be part of God's plan.

And there's another thing that confirms us in that view. It's to do with what God is *like*. If the Bible teaches us anything about God, surely it's that he is 100 per cent good! God is neither evil in himself nor given to causing evil. He is kind, merciful, loving and compassionate. So once again, it looks like there are some big question marks about drawing any kind of line between life's hardships and God.

But if that's the case, how on earth are we to explain the fact that we live in such a troubled world? Why are there earthquakes, cyclones and floods? Where do leukaemia, MS and Downs Syndrome come from? What about bereavement, depression and panic attacks?

We've got to take seriously both the plans of God and the goodness of God on the one hand, and – on the other – the fact of human suffering. And here's how we do it. Consciously or subconsciously, this is the equation we've come up with.

God's ideal world was pain-free

+

God is not evil

+

Bad things happen

=

God is not ultimately responsible for them

The way we express the equation will vary. Perhaps the most common is that, while we're happy to talk about obvious blessings as *sent* or *given* by God (as in 'look at our beautiful baby God has *given* us'), we're likely to speak of suffering in a slightly different way. We'll say that it's just *allowed* or *permitted* by him (as in 'why would God *allow* Tom to die at such a young age?'). Do you spot the difference there?

As we'll see in the next chapter, this way of talking does preserve an important truth. We quite rightly don't want to say anything that might imply God is himself evil. That would be intolerable. The problem is: the Bible isn't quite as squeamish as us. God and painful things *do* often get linked together – and very closely at that! So it turns out that the way we speak in fact represents something of a retreat from how the Bible often talks about God.

The God of our hearts, then, has been further downgraded from the Bible's portrait of him. We haven't just got him switching between cruise control and manual as he sees fit; there are now a whole range of situations in which – as a matter of *course* – he doesn't intervene.

THE RESPECTFUL GOD

You can lead a horse to water, so the saying goes, but you can't make him drink. I can't say I've tried it with a horse, but my limited experience with cats, dogs and babies makes me pretty confident that the saying holds true!

But is it true of God and human beings? Does God content himself with simply holding out an open invitation to a relationship with him?

He certainly does that much. 'Come, everyone who thirsts', we read in Isaiah 55. 'Come to the waters... Seek the Lord while he may be found, call upon him while he is near.' God is inviting his people to respond to him and receive life and forgiveness. But is that as far it goes? Does his work finish when he's put that offer on the table? Does he just sit back and wait for us to bite, all the while keeping his distance and respecting our personal space?

Certainly many believe so, and it's not hard to see why. Absolute, unconstrained freedom to determine one's own future is seen by the world as an essential ingredient of personhood. It's part of what it means to be human. We recoil against the idea of someone else deciding our future. It might be in our political life – ditching dictators and replacing them with a liberal democracy, so that our national life is decided by the will of the people. Or it could be in our personal lives – think about a film like *Minority Report* with its premise of the future being so fixed that – thanks to predictive technology – future criminals are caught and punished before they even commit their crime. We recoil against a prospect like this! Unqualified freedom is a driving force for the world and specifically for what we think it means to be human.

Most of us – when we become Christians – bring a decent-sized slice of that worldview with us into the way we think about our spiritual lives. And it can often be quite a while (and involve a long, hard struggle) before we ditch it.

After all, there are plenty of Bible verses that seem at first sight to support us in our take on these things. There are places that show God apparently content to leave key spiritual decisions entirely to us without influencing us in any way. We're told to repent and believe – and it certainly sounds as though it's down to us whether we do or not. We learn that God wants everyone to be saved – which suggests he's content to put the invitation out and leave it at that. We see people deciding whether or not to respond to Christ based on whether they're convinced by other people's attempts to persuade – making it sound like a matter for rational human thought-processes. We even come across people who apparently used to believe but have decided (for whatever reason) to backtrack – which fits the bill perfectly for fickle, blow-hot-and-cold human beings, but not God! We really do feel quite justified in seeing our spiritual futures as completely in our hands.

But if that's where we are, it's important to realise what we're doing. We're putting ourselves firmly back in the God-shrinking business. Not only does he take his hands off the controls when there's any kind of pain involved; now he lets things take their own course when it involves a human decision – especially when it's a decision that involves spiritual things. And that's a massive demotion for God.

THE GRANDMASTER GOD

May 11 1997 was a watershed moment in the world of chess. It was the first time in history that a reigning world champion was defeated by a computer. IBM's 'Deep Blue' went up against Gary Kasparov and managed – largely by sheer number-crunching power – to come out on top. It was able to weigh up 200 million potential moves per second, and so plan a response to whatever Kasparov did, sometimes up to twenty moves ahead. It had an answer for everything, and proved it by securing the victory, much to the dismay of Kasparov (who claimed foul play, saying that a human must have helped the computer at points).

Could God be to human beings what 'Deep Blue' is to its opponent?

We've already seen some fairly massive reductions in the stature of God as the Bible presents him. He's taken some big hits in terms of his activity in the world. But there's one thing he's still kept hold of. His control may have diminished, but so far at least his knowledge is still intact. Even if he's not micro-managing every detail of the universe's existence, he at least – on the versions of God we've looked at to this point – knows how it's going to unravel.

Not any more. In recent decades, some within the Christian fold have started to wonder whether he even knows what's around the corner. If we're going to be serious about people being completely free to decide their future without any interference from God, then God can't know what's going to happen. Because if you know something ahead of time, you're actually – they say – controlling it. Why's that? Think about it. If God already knows today how you're going to spend next Sunday afternoon, then how can you wake up next Sunday morning and make a completely spontaneous, free decision about what you're going to do later on that day? It's already set. It's already decided in some way. Otherwise how could it have been known? If someone already knows what you're going to decide, it means your decision can't be a completely independent, autonomous one.

So we've no option left to us. If people are going to be truly free, divine foreknowledge has to go. Instead, God is like a cosmic chess grandmaster (a God-sized 'Deep Blue') playing any number of games at once with different people around the world. The final outcome is not in doubt: he's going to win every one of them. He will get to where he wants to go. Why? Because he's very, very good. But the route to his victory is completely unpredictable. He doesn't know what the next move will be on any of the boards. And so he simply has to wait and see what the human being on the other side of the table does, then make the best response of all the potential counter-moves available to him. He can make sure it ends in the right way; he just can't control how it gets there, because he never knows what's coming.

Some philosophers and theologians like this version of God. It allows them to hold on to the idea of a 'Higher Being', while not denting 'human self-realisation'. But something like it is not that uncommon among ordinary Christians too, especially when we come to make decisions. There is a tendency in some of us to worry about getting our guidance so wrong that we 'fall out of God's will'. And so we start to wonder if God can ever get us back on track. But when we worry like this, we're laying our cards on the table about our view of God. We're saying we've taken him by surprise; that he wasn't prepared for this turn of events. And now the invisible grandmaster facing us has got his work cut out if he's going to figure out how to get the game of our lives back on towards the right outcome.

Whether it's as deep-thinking theologians or as ordinary Christians, though, there's no doubt that our God has just got a lot smaller. To abandon foreknowledge as well as control is yet another major downgrade. Indeed there's not all that much further to go before the shrinkage journey reaches its terminus. Just one final stop.

THE BIG BANG GOD

Alice in Wonderland is a strange book, in which strange conversations take place between strange characters. Strangest of all, though, is the Cheshire cat. It pops up from time to time to engage Alice in bizarre lines of conversation, leaving her puzzled, or just plain infuriated. But it also has an inexplicable tendency to fade away and disappear – either quickly or more gradually. As it goes, though, there is one part of its anatomy that lingers even after the rest of it has vanished from sight. It is the cat's trademark mischievous grin. Tail, body, legs, ears and even the rest of the face go; all that is left is that grin.

This is effectively the point we've got to in our look at God. We've seen how God's sway over the unfolding of history (and particularly human history) gets increasingly whittled away by the various different takes on him. But some would go further and say God doesn't involve himself in the day-to-day realities of the world *at all*. He still exists, but his last genuine involvement with the world was when he brought the cosmos into being. It's as though he wound up the clock, got it going but then left it – full of potential – to tick away. Or – in terms of the picture we used earlier in this chapter – not only has he hit the cruise control button, he's promptly abandoned the driving seat and got out of the car, leaving it to work out its own route based solely on the direction it was pointing at in the beginning.

There is, then, only the tiniest glimmer of God's activity still to be seen in the world – nothing but the grin of the Cheshire Cat, you might say. The order and natural laws of the universe are the last reminder we have that he even exists.

This view of God certainly has its attractions. It offers an easy explanation, for example, of why the suffering we see in the world seems to be so indiscriminate. God is just not involved any more. The universe is completely closed off to any such meddling from outside. So the blame for the pain cannot be left at God's door.

It also makes God wonderfully undemanding. Nobody's going to have to give account to him for the way they've lived their lives. There is no day of reckoning to come. God's work is over and done with. He is no more than an explanation for our cosmic past. He doesn't impact our present or our future. So we can relax and get on with life the way we want.

Maybe that's why this version of God is so popular. Because it really is. It's not just scientists looking for an explanation of the Big Bang who are happy with this kind of 'flick-the-first-domino-and-scarper' God. Millions of people believe in God, according to the censuses. But the God they believe in has only a minimal impact on their lives. They're rarely – if ever – to be found in church. Their values, ambitions, priorities and dreams show no evidence of being impacted by the Bible. Their lives are virtually indistinguishable from an unbeliever. They believe in God – just not a God who has anything to do with their lives or indeed the world at large.

It's not hard to see why this approach to God is so appealing in the world. It solves that sneaking suspicion so many have that there is some kind of Higher Force behind the world, while at the same time not actually demanding that we change our lives one iota.

But of course it also virtually strips God bare. Not only is there no control or foreknowledge left in him. There is no love, care, mercy, compassion or indeed anything else 'personal' about him. This 'God' is more a fact than a father. He cannot speak or answer prayer. He's not interested in directing history or guiding individuals. He's not moved by either beautiful self-sacrifice or horrendous atrocities. He offers no hope of a new future. Indeed he is not really a 'he' at all; more just an 'it'.

One thing's for sure. We're now a million miles from the God of the Bible.

ৡ

Did you recognise your God somewhere among the contenders I mentioned?

There are all sorts of factors that drive us to step back from the way the Bible presents God. There may be intellectual issues. We struggle with how this or that verse fits in with the overall picture of God. Or there might be evangelistic motivations. We want to go with a version of God we feel we can defend to someone who doesn't yet believe in him at all. Or it might just come down to the environment we're in. Everyone in our particular Christian circles seem to assume this or that about God, and we don't want to rock the boat or risk relationships or perhaps just expend the mental energy required. So we just go with the flow.

But none of those is the really big factor. The really, really big factor that tends to lie behind God-shrinkage is the question of where *we* fit in the scheme of things.

IT'S ALL ABOUT ME!
Let me tell you a little parable.

Tim loved his new house. It was a brand new place – the architect, who had supervised the entire building work, had just signed off on it. And it was a big, minimalist, open plan sort of building. Its big feature was the way it was completely wrapped around with glass. The walls were just massive windows. Even the ceiling had a huge skylight in it. The whole place was full of light. It was very impressive.

Another feature of the house was a little flowerbed right in the middle of it. And in the middle of the flowerbed was one little plant: it was a gift left there by the architect himself. The great thing was: it needed hardly any attention. The flowerbed had a fully plumbed-in, automated watering system. And, of course, there was plenty of light in the house. All that was required was a little pruning from time to time to keep it from getting out of control – it was potentially quite a vigorous grower if not tended to in this way.

But Tim's friends weren't so sure about this low-maintenance approach. They encouraged Tim to water it regularly just to make sure, so he did. The magazines Tim read were full of advertisements for different types of artificial fertiliser recommended for that kind of plant. So Tim decided to try some of these too. And the TV gardening programmes said it really wasn't a great idea to prune those plants – they needed to be able to grow naturally. So Tim followed that advice too.

And it made a difference. Within weeks, it was shooting up and the leaves were thickening. Within a few months, it was already pushing the bounds for a normal-sized houseplant. Any more growth and it would be out of proportion. But still Tim carried on with his 'extra water, artificial fertiliser, zero-pruning' regime. After all, he didn't want it to die!

The thing about plants is that, if you see them every day, you don't really notice the growth. It's not until someone comes to visit you that you get an outside perspective and realise just how they've shot up. And so it was that it took a visit from the architect himself – he shamelessly invited himself around for tea a year on – for Tim to realise just what had happened and how different the house had come to look.

Because by then the change was dramatic. That little plant had grown to the point where its branches filled the entire house. The root structure was so developed that there was noticeable subsidence. And getting around the house, even from the kitchen to the living area, involved stepping over some branches, ducking others and generally some pretty impressive acrobatics. The plant had come to dominate everything.

But the change which concerned the architect most of all was the light. Or rather the lack of it. The foliage was so dense that barely any of that beautiful light was getting through. If you looked really carefully, you could see a kind of pale tinge around the edge of some of the leaves. But that was now about all you could see of the light. It had become a dark green. This was really not what the architect had envisaged.

Time to unpack the parable?

The house is your mind – or mine.

The architect is, of course, God, as he shows himself to us in his word. As children of God, our minds are to be shaped first and foremost by the word of God.

The light flooding into the house is the awareness we're given of God's wise and good purposes being worked out in the world. When things are as they should be, this awareness colours every area of our thinking. It casts its light into every little crevice of our minds.

The plant is how we think of our ability to shape our lives and the world around us. It's real, this ability. We genuinely have the power to change things. And so it has a right place in our thinking. But it's only part of the picture. And it's completely dependent on God: he gave it to us, and he provides the light and the water it needs. It does have the potential to get out of proportion, to grow into total, full-blown human autonomy. So it does need to be kept in check with the occasional application of some pruning shears. But the world around us – friends, TV and media, for example – constantly encourage us only to cultivate this sense of our own ability to determine things (the fertiliser). And not to keep it in check (no pruning).

And that's exactly what we do, to different degrees. We let it grow. And it's the main reason why the light of God's rule over our lives gets dimmed. Why the God of our minds shrinks. *God* gets smaller because *we* get bigger.

Unshrinking the God of our Hearts

The year is 1543 and one of the most learned men of the Renaissance period is lying on his deathbed. His various careers have included military leader, governor, lawyer, doctor, clergyman, diplomat, economist and mathematician. He is a true genius. But he won't be remembered much for his work in any of these areas. Instead he will be remembered for the fruit of his labours in what was really just a hobby to him. Minutes before his death, so the story goes, he is handed the first printed copy of his book, hot off the press. He smiles and slips peacefully away. But that book which brings a smile to the face of its dying author, Nicolaus Copernicus, will prove to be dynamite in the world at large. It will become one of the greatest landmarks of modern science.

The book was called *On the Orbits of the Celestial Bodies*. If you think that's not the catchiest of titles, you should check out the original Latin. Title aside, though, the great aim of the book was to prove as fact what seemed a most bizarre and unlikely-sounding idea. It was that the earth was not in fact the centre of the universe; it was, rather, just a satellite of the sun, spinning around it along with the other planets. If you wanted to know what the hub of everything was, he said, that would be the sun.

And so was born what became known as the Copernican revolution. It was all about revolution: the earth's revolutions around the sun. But more than that, it was a revolution in itself – a revolution in the way we thought about our existence. Suddenly we were not at the centre. Something else was.

Many Christians today have more than a little in common with the contemporaries of Copernicus 500 years ago, at least as far as the spiritual analogy goes. We believe in God, just as they believed in the sun. In that sense, we've seen the light! We acknowledge God's great power, just as they were well aware of the energy emanating from the sun. We appreciate the blessings that flow to us from God, just as they appreciated what the sun did for them. Indeed, we rely on God, we trust in him, we acknowledge that we could not live without him, just as people then knew perfectly well how much they depended on the sun for their survival.

But that is not necessarily to say that he is, for us, truly the centre around whom we revolve, dictating the course of our lives – any more than the people of Copernicus' day saw the sun as the gravitational centre for the earth's movement. It is quite possible for me to be a Christian but still effectively to think and operate in some ways as though things really revolve around me.

It's time to spell out what I'm trying to achieve in this book. For one thing, I want to help you to discover some of the ways in which you may have conceived of God as something other than the gravitational centre of history and indeed your individual life. Then I want to enable you to get your mind around just how it's possible for God to be truly in the driving seat with his hands firmly on the controls, given all that you see and experience in your life which seems to suggest otherwise. And third, I want to show something of the difference it will make to your daily spiritual walk when you begin to recognise God as truly God.

In this chapter, we're moving on from the first aim to the second. This is where we ask: how is it possible to be totally intellectually honest and consistent and still accept the portrait of God which the Bible presents? Or, to put it another way, how can we fit the various pieces of the jigsaw together so that we see clearly how God can stand behind *everything* in our lives and the world as a whole and yet we're not just puppets? Or to put it yet another way, how can we reverse the shrinkage process that we saw in the last chapter and rescale the God of our hearts upwards, without just saying 'I don't know' to all the questions and challenges of those who've opted for a more diminished God?

In the chapters that follow, we'll be returning to some of the specific areas of the Christian life which many struggle with. We'll look at big questions about suffering, prayer, decision-making and evangelism. But if we're going to be able to build up our thinking in those areas, we first need to lay a solid foundation.

And here's where to begin.

HUMBLE HEARTS AND MALLEABLE MINDS

It's been said that the only people who like change are babies with dirty nappies – and even they tend to cry about it. I reckon that's not too far off the mark. For every entrepreneur, innovator and early adopter, there seem to be ten who are far less keen to adapt their lives to the new fashion, or gadget or life-reality. We like what we're used to, by and large.

Sadly, the same holds true of our opinions and the way we think. The longer we've been committed to a position, and the greater the number of life-moments that position has helped us to think through, and the more people we've articulated that position to – the harder it is to rethink it. In practice, that means that – as a general rule – the longer you've lived (past the age of, say, twenty), the trickier it will be for you to change your mind about anything!

But there are some areas of thinking that are *even harder* than usual to revisit. They're the areas that affect your whole approach to life – questions to do with religion and worldview. Unfortunately, what we're looking at in this chapter, and indeed the book as a whole, is one such area. It has to do with a question as basic as 'how free am I?'

If you're a film-goer (with a long memory), you may be able to think of a number of big-screen characters who've struggled with these questions.

First, there was Truman Burbank. Remember him? *The Truman Show* told the story of his dawning realisation that his life was in fact constructed and orchestrated by somebody else. When the penny finally drops, his mind is sent into turmoil and he becomes desperate to try to escape his phony existence.

Then there was Neo, in *The Matrix*, famously swallowing the red pill and having his eyes opened to the reality that all human experience was just simulated reality. The truth was that human beings were simply an energy source for the machines which held them in slavery. Neo made it his quest to fight for freedom against these machines.

More recently, *The Adjustment Bureau* saw congressman David Norris bristling at the idea that his relationship with the only woman he has ever really loved is to be ended because it is not part of the predetermined 'plan' for his life. He won't stand for it and promptly decides to fight this destiny using nothing but the brute force of his own love-struck willpower.

These are just a few of the films that explore issues of human freedom and determination. That it is such a common subject only serves to underline how deeply such themes resonate with us. The thought of being mere puppets in someone else's show, or pawns being moved around some great chessboard, is an outrage to us.

There's a reason why we – even we believers – shrink God down in terms of his impact on us. It's that we don't want someone else messing with our world. And we certainly don't want him messing with our heads.

That's the starting point for many of us. It's where we are. And if we're going to reboot our worldview with an upgraded version of God in it, we're not going to find it easy. We need to pray for a humble heart and a malleable mind.

It takes a heroic dose of humility to acknowledge – even to ourselves – that we may have been operating with a defective view of God. But humility is not a new idea to the Christian. It is something that our great saviour the Lord Jesus modelled to us in the most powerful way imaginable, when he 'humbled himself by becoming obedient to the point of death – even death on a cross' (Phil. 2:8). And it is something God's word commands: 'Humble yourselves, therefore, under the mighty hand of God, so that at the proper time he may exalt you' (1 Pet. 5:6).

And humility leads naturally into malleability. Once we've acknowledged the possibility that we may have misconstrued God in the past, the next thing for us to do is to nurture a determination to be shaped by his word in the future. 'Do not be conformed to the world', says the apostle Paul, 'but be transformed by the renewal of your mind...' (Rom. 12:2). When was the last time you changed your mind about some area of biblical truth? Go on: think about it. Discipline yourself right now not to read on until you've answered that question!

The comedian Jerry Seinfeld used to joke about how closed we are to making new friends after we get to a certain age. 'We ought to put up a sign', he said. 'Sorry, we're not hiring!' The sad thing is that many Christians in practice do a similar thing with truth. We may as well put up a sign too: 'Sorry, we're not learning'.

Can I encourage you, as you read on, to cultivate in yourself – in the power of the Spirit of God – a truly humble heart, one that's ready, if need be, to confess to having got it wrong before? And can I urge you too to approach what follows with a genuinely malleable mind, one that's open to being challenged by the word of God to rethink your views, rather than use your existing 'system' as a kind of spiritual TEFLON that means new insights from the Bible never really stick?

GO LARGE

With that attitude of heart and mind in place, we're ready to lay down some of the key building blocks for a robust biblical view of God's activity in the world today.

But first, let me ask you a question. It's one that might seem a bit beside the point, but bear with me! Is light a wave or a particle? If you've got a scientific background, you'll probably be able to answer that question more articulately and maybe with some longer words than those of us who don't have that background. But the answer, as I understand it at least, is: well, it's kind of both!

Ever since the rise of quantum physics, it's been accepted that there are some ways light acts like a wave, and some ways it behaves more like a particle. Now that's a pretty inconvenient answer for people who like everything neat and tidy. We'd much prefer if it was one or the other. We'd like to put it in a box and label it so that every instance of light anywhere in the cosmos always conformed to a pre-packaged set of rules. But it turns out it's just not like that. Troublesome as it may be to physicists and people who think about such things, they can't take a single, flat approach to light. They need to think about it in two different ways at the same time if they're going to understand it properly.

If we're to grasp how God works in the world today, and what that means for us, we need to apply that same 'unflattening' approach to three key subjects: (1) God's will, (2) human will and (3) the way that God's will rubs up against ours.

UNFLATTENING GOD'S WILL

There's a reason why many of us have either tied ourselves in mental knots on these questions or else contented ourselves with a small view of God. That reason is that we've never really grappled properly with how the Bible talks about the will of God. We've never got beyond thinking in a 'flat' way. Whenever we come across God decreeing, ordaining, sending, promising, desiring, or commanding anything, we take such verses as though they're about pretty much the same thing – basically what God wants. That is, we approach these parts of the Bible as though they were just a whole series of pieces of the same pie – the 'will of God' pie.

But they aren't. We can't think about the will of God in just one, flat way – any more than we can think about light like that. We need to understand God's will in two different ways.

On the one hand, there is God's *ideal*. This is what he would like for the world and for us human beings if human sinfulness were not a factor. He would like us to be like him – truly the 'image of God' that we were made to be. And he would like us to be in perfect relationship with him – the 'bride' of Christ that we will together one day be.

That's not how it is, though. The reality is that, ever since Adam and Eve ate the forbidden fruit, sin has indeed been a factor. And not just one factor, but a *defining* influence. Apart from God's Spirit, we cannot help but rebel against God: we are slaves to the power of sin. Even for those who have had their chains cut off by God's work in their lives, sin remains a daily reality. It may not have any actual, constitutional power any more, but it has a loud and alluring voice which, to our great shame, we find ourselves following time and again of our own free choice.

And so, because of the reality of sin, God's ideal-will can be defied. In fact, it's defied routinely in the world. And it will continue to be defied until the whole created order is brought low before the throne of Christ. God's ideal-will is about what *should* be in the world, and what *will be* in the new creation. But it's not necessarily what *is* in the here and now.

What sort of places do we look to find out about God's ideal-will? Well, the Bible's a big book, but here are just a few examples.

'Therefore a man shall leave his father and mother and hold fast to his wife; and they shall become one flesh.' (Gen. 2:24)

'Whoever oppresses a poor man insults his Maker, but he who is generous to the needy honours him.' (Prov. 14:31)

'If anyone would come after me, let him deny himself, and take up his cross daily and follow me.' (Luke 9:23)

'But as he who called you is holy, you also be holy in all your conduct.' (1 Pet. 1:15)

'But the fruit of the Spirit is love, joy, peace, patience, kindness, goodness, faithfulness, gentleness, self-control.' (Gal. 5:22-23)

These are all part of God's ideal for us as his creatures: that our marriages last, that we take care of others, that we follow Jesus, that we pursue holiness and that our characters have a specific Christ-like shape to them. There are hundreds more examples we could very easily come up with. These will have to do for now.

They come in different forms, but each of them opens a window for us to see the will of God, in the sense of what God loves to see. That's God's ideal-will.

On the other hand, there is the will of God that might best be described as his *plan*. This is not necessarily what he approves of. It's what he decides – for reasons we may not always understand – is going to happen. It includes big things and small – God is a macro-manager as well as a micro-manager. And it includes things both wonderful and terrible, both joyful and heart-breaking, things which bring honour to him and his son Jesus and things which really don't.

The thing about God's plan-will is that it *always* comes to pass. There are no ifs or buts. No exceptions. There's a straight line from God's plan to history. If you want to know what God's plan was for yesterday, think back to what you thought and felt. Ask your friends how they spent the day. Read a newspaper. Whatever actually happened yesterday – that was God's plan.

If you want to know what God's plan is for tomorrow, it's... No, sorry, we're not that lucky! God doesn't reveal the details of his plan-will ahead of time. We get some very general clues about what he's going to do between now and when Jesus returns. For example, he's going to assemble the cast for the action of the new creation (ie call people to himself and build up the church). And he's going to get us ready for what's to come (ie grow us in Christian maturity). But advance copies of the detailed blueprint are not available.

And yes, in case you were wondering, it is impossible to go against God's plan-will. That's partly because we don't know what it is. But even if we did, it's not open for discussion. There's no triumph of the human free spirit here – that's just for the big screen. When it comes to God's plan-will, what God wants in this sense, God gets.

Of course, that does beg a few questions about how prayer changes things (because it does!) and how the decisions we make can affect anything (because they do!). We'll come to that. But for now, the whole point about God's plan-will is that it can't be foiled or frustrated.

How does the Bible express this idea about God having a set plan? Again, in various ways.

David acknowledges that God had worked out his diary for him before he was even born: 'In your book were written, every one of them, the days that were formed for me, when as yet there were none of them' (Ps. 139:16).

Proverbs makes very clear that we can't fight against God's plan and win: 'There is no wisdom, no insight, no plan that can succeed against the LORD' (Prov. 21:30, NIV).

The link between God's decisions and history, Isaiah is told, is cast-iron: 'As I have planned, so shall it be, and as I have purposed, so shall it stand' (Isa. 14:24).

Jesus himself assures his followers that the plan includes even the tiniest details of people's lives: 'Are not two sparrows sold for a penny? And not one of them will fall to the ground apart from the will of your Father. But even the hairs of your head are all numbered' (Matt. 10:29-30).

And, crucially, he says, it even includes who will or won't respond to God. 'No one can come to me unless the Father who sent me draws him' (John 6:44).

So God's plan-will is exhaustive and it's unstoppable. It's gritty and real. Where God's ideal-will is all about what should be, God's plan-will is about what was, what is and what will be.

You can see why, when we're talking about the will of God, we've got to be clear on the sense we're talking about! But doesn't this turn God into a schizophrenic? If God really has two wills which often completely contradict each other, surely we're now dealing with some kind of Dr Jekyll and Mr Hyde?

That's certainly how it might seem. But just think about it for a moment. We actually have different wills in all sorts of situations.

As a teacher, I might have wanted to encourage a struggling pupil by giving him a good mark – perhaps higher than what was in front of me deserved. But I also wanted to keep him from getting complacent and to be fair to the rest of the class. One teacher; two wills.

As a parent, I might like to enjoy a nice, quiet meal with my family, with none of the sort of screaming and crying that usually goes with my young child being made to eat an unfamiliar food. But I also want to make sure my child doesn't grow up to be a fussy eater. One parent; two wills.

As a manager, I might want to get my pound of flesh out of my employees, keeping them working all hours to be as productive as possible. But I also want my employees to enjoy their work, to have a balanced life and to remain motivated. One manager; two wills.

So we know at least a little of what it's like to 'will' different things at the same time in the same situation. It's not a new concept to us. Of course, it's not *quite* the same for God himself. But let's face it. Do we really expect to understand the inner workings of the divine mind? 'As the heavens are higher than the earth', says God, 'so are my ways higher than your ways and my thoughts than your thoughts' (Isa. 55:9, NIV).

So there's the first idea that we need to get our heads around – the idea that God's will is not one simple, single thing, but needs to be thought about in two different ways.

If we don't grasp this – if we stay with a 'flat' view of God's will – we will never get how things can happen which we know God disapproves of. We'll assume that God couldn't have done anything about them.

Now it's time to come a bit closer to home.

UNFLATTENING THE HUMAN WILL
Remaking the great films of old is a precarious business. Witness attempts like *Godzilla*, *Poseidon* and *The Pink*

Panther. So the mixed reviews of *The Italian Job* remake were hardly surprising. But it does contain a scene which may help ease us into the subject at hand.

It's a heist movie, in which one of a gang of robbers turns on his colleagues after a 'job'. He kills one, leaves the others for dead and takes the gold for himself. The survivors then make it their business to recover the loot. With obvious references to the original film, the plan involves a bunch of Minis, a Londoner, and – of course – a carefully orchestrated traffic jam. The jam is naturally unnerving to the driver of the armoured car containing the gold, and so he looks for a way through. At junction after junction he makes a decision about which way to go: left, right or straight on. But here's the strange thing. Despite making a whole series of perfectly free choices, he eventually arrives at the exact spot his former colleagues have earmarked for their ambush.

How so? Because, as we viewers can see from our all-knowing perspective, one of the ambush team is working behind the scenes. With exclusive access to the city's traffic light network and its traffic cameras, he can both see and control everything. He gives a series of green lights at each junction as the armoured car approaches. Each of them is only valid for one direction and so effectively ensures the driver goes that way and nowhere else.

As far as the driver's concerned, he's making perfectly free decisions: every step of the way, he evaluates the options and chooses what he thinks is the best way forward. He could easily choose some other course, and if he does, it really will lead to a different route and different consequences. But the bigger picture shows that, while each of those *choices* is indeed free, there is a higher power involved in the background which makes sure the driver's free choices end up going a particular way.

It's not a perfect illustration, but it does capture something of the paradox of the Bible's answer to the question: 'do we have free will or not?' The answer is yes and no! Yes, we make free choices. We really can go either way at the various crossroads in life we come to. And so, rightly, we'll be held to account if we do what's morally wrong. But no, the minds with which we make those choices are most certainly not independent of God. Our thinking processes are not God-free zones.

Does that bug you? Does it make you bristle? Does it sound like just a fudge? You'd be unusual if it didn't make you react in at least one of those ways! Because let's face it, at any given moment, it certainly feels like we're free – and free all the way through. Remember, though, what we saw before about 'humble hearts and malleable minds'. The message we hear all around us each day is that we create our own destiny, that we're characters in our own play. Our own experience and intuition may seem to chime in with that message. But God's word says something different.

One of the biggest moments in the whole of the Old Testament was the time when the descendants of Jacob made an exit from Egypt and became a nation in their own right. What was a bunch of runaway slaves were formed into a people with their own constitution and laws, their own lifestyle and identity, and eventually their own land. But the story of how that came to be involved some high drama. Moses asked Pharaoh repeatedly for permission to take his people out into the desert. But again and again the answer was no – this despite a series of fairly impressive attempts at persuasion.

The question is: how did Pharaoh reach that decision? Why did he say no? On one level, he simply chose what he thought was right – after all, he'd be kissing his workforce goodbye if he gave in. So he 'hardened his heart and would not listen to them'. But there was a bigger picture. It turns out the Pharaoh's mind was not as free as he might have thought. 'You shall speak all that I command you', God had said to Moses, '...but I will harden Pharaoh's heart, and though I multiply my signs and wonders in the land of Egypt, Pharaoh will not listen to you' (Exod. 7:2-4).

It turns out, then, that God was behind everything. He was planning all along for Israel to go out in the extraordinary way they eventually did. Pharaoh's obstinacy was part of the plan.

This is just one example among many where we see the Proverbs 21:1 principle being acted out in real life: 'The king's heart is a stream of water in the hands of the LORD; he turns it wherever he will.' That is, even the most powerful people on the planet aren't immune to having their minds being influenced by God.

Think about King Sihon of Heshbon, for example. OK, he may not be someone you find yourself thinking about too often. So in case your memory's a little hazy on the details of his case, allow me to remind you. The people of Israel were travelling in the wilderness and came up against the border of Heshbon. Trying to be peaceable, Moses duly applied for a transit visa so that the people could travel through. 'Let me pass through your land. I will go only by the road; I will turn aside neither to the right nor to the left' (Deut. 2:27).

But King Sihon refused the application. Maybe he was worried about their intentions. Maybe there were other political reasons. We don't know. But as he weighed up the benefits (possibilities for trade with the travellers) against the risks, he came down on the negative side. Once again, though, there was a bigger picture: '...Sihon the king of Heshbon would not let us pass by him, for the Lord your God hardened his spirit and made his heart obstinate, that he might give him into your hand...' (v. 30).

So God was there in the background. We don't know the mechanics of how God got his way. But we do know that he was at work in the king's mind. This king's heart, for one, was a 'stream of water in the hands of the Lord'.

The same could be said of Absalom when he was going after David. Two advisers offered him and his people contradictory strategies. He listened to them both, weighed them up and made his decision. 'Absalom and all the men of Israel said, "The counsel of Hushai the Archite is better than the counsel of Ahithophel."' But again, Absalom's mind was not free from God's influence. Immediately we're given the bigger, but hidden, reality of the situation. Absalom went that way because 'the LORD had ordained to defeat the good counsel of Ahithophel, so that the LORD might bring harm upon Absalom' (2 Sam. 17:14).

It's the same story over and over again – people going a particular way on some decision or other – making significant decisions which were real choices, but which came from a mind influenced by God.

Before the Israelites left Egypt, they brazenly asked their Egyptian neighbours for silver and gold. Strangely enough, they all said yes. Why? Because 'the LORD had given the people favour in the sight of the Egyptians, so that they let them have what they asked' (Exod. 12:36). When Daniel and his friends start their three-year training course in Babylon, Daniel's outrageous request to be served a special menu every day is granted. Why? Because 'God gave Daniel favour and compassion in the sight of his supervisor' (Dan. 1:9). When Cyrus woke up one morning thinking about his territories, he came up with the idea to commission the rebuilding of the temple in Jerusalem. Why? Ultimately because 'the LORD stirred up the spirit of Cyrus' to do exactly that (Ezra 1:1).

There can be no doubt about it: at a deep level, our minds are shaped by God. And yes, that even goes for non-rational impulses – like sexual attraction. We don't know an awful lot about the early life of the great Samson. The Bible account skips from his birth to puberty in just two verses. The first real glimpse we have of the details of his life is a hormonally-charged moment.

'Samson went down to Timnah, and at Timnah he saw one of the daughters of the Philistines.' That one sighting, it seems, was enough. He was smitten. And – much to the consternation of Mum and Dad – he knew exactly what he wanted. 'Samson said to his father, "Get her for me, for she is right in my eyes"' (Judg. 14:1-3).

There's not much more personal, you'd think, than sexual attraction. 'Beauty is in the eye of the beholder', we say. But in reality, even this is ultimately up to God. Samson's infatuation with this foreign girl, it turns out in the next verse, was 'from the Lord, for he was seeking an opportunity against the Philistines'.

But we haven't yet come to the most important example of a course of action both freely chosen and yet decided upon by a mind shaped by forces outside itself. That title must go to the decision to come to trust and obey God or not.

'Choose this day whom you will serve', said Joshua. 'Follow me', said Jesus. 'Repent and believe', said Peter.

These were real decisions being called for. And an awful lot hung on the response. But the minds of those called upon to make those decisions – both then and now – are not blank slates. Far from it. They're described as 'blinded', 'enslaved', even 'dead'. Their eyes need to be opened, they need to be set free and they need to be made alive – in every case by something or someone outside themselves.

So the 'will' of human beings needs to be put under the microscope just as the will of God does. And – again like the will of God – it turns out to be a catch-all word: it needs to be separated out into the choices we make – real, authentic, make-a-difference choices – and the mind that makes them – shaped and moulded by the power of God.

HOW GOD'S WILL AND OURS RELATE TO EACH OTHER

Let me ask you a question. How would you explain what a kiss is? How's this for a definition: 'the anatomical juxtaposition of two *orbicularis oris* muscles in a state of contraction'? Or is it just a way of saying 'I love you'?

Why am I feeling hungry? Is it because my liver is responding to a low level of glucose in my blood and signalling as much to my lateral hypothalamus? Or is it just that it's been a few hours since I last ate and somebody near me is stuffing themselves with a warm blueberry muffin?

What's the reason that so many divorces happen in the Western world today? Is it because of abuse, infidelity, unrealistic expectations, financial conflict, lack of commitment, and the like? Or is that people just aren't living according to the maker's instructions?

In each case, one reality is being described in two quite different ways.

Earlier in this chapter, I mentioned that light doesn't quite fit the neat categories some scientists might have liked. It needs to be looked at in a couple of different ways. We saw that God's will is like that, and the human will too. But more than that, even the relationship between the two needs to be thought of in this two-layered way.

The common, 'flat' way of thinking about the relationship says that God is responsible for certain things in the world, and indeed my life, and then we're responsible for the rest. That is, there are certain pieces in the jigsaw of my life that God puts in place, but the rest are down to me (and perhaps people I interact with) to decide.

How much is there of each? We'll probably disagree on that. Maybe God just gets the corner pieces in place. Maybe all the edges too. Maybe whole sections of the jigsaw puzzle, leaving just a few blank spots for me to fill in. But the point is: it's a bit of him and a bit of me.

So, for example, God decides that Beth is going to become one of his children. But the 'how and when' details of her conversion are up for grabs. Who will it be that shares the gospel with her? How long will she take to wrestle with the issues? What will be the final clincher that destroys her defences and leads her to get on her knees before her heavenly father? Those are all details that God's happy to leave Beth and people around her to work out – according to the 'flat' view of God's will.

Or God decides that Peter and Lisa are going to be married. God decides that he's going to bless Peter and Lisa with children. And God gifts Peter and Lisa for the ministry they take on in their church. But when the marriage disintegrates into endless and unbearable bickering, leaving him vulnerable to the affair which he embarks on, resulting in his deciding to walk out on his wife and lose interest in his children – that would be all Peter. God is nowhere near any of that. How could he be?

Or God was completely behind one of the two new outreach ministries the church Jim attends started last year. But not the other. The new Friday night community youth group was definitely God. People prayed, the church caught the vision, the money came in, and the young people flocked to the venue week by week. But the 'help the homeless' initiative was certainly not God. Nobody wanted it. The leadership only agreed to it because they were manipulated into it. It was all about Jim. He wanted to be the great hero, bringing a social conscience for the church and a name for himself. The ministry has just been limping along. The common consensus is that God's not in it; it's all Jim.

The idea is that some things are of God; other things are of us. And it's a pretty common way of thinking. But it's not a biblical way of thinking.

You can certainly find verses which – taken on their own – sound like they're supporting this flat, 'either God or us' view of things. But when you look at them closely, you realise they're talking only about God's ideal-will, not his plan-will.

The truth is that the things which happen in our lives are all down to us, and all down to God, at the very same time. It's not either-or; it's both-and! Even the trivial things, even the bad things, even the things that happen as a result of the worst possible motivations. Like the kiss, or hunger, or relationship breakdowns, one reality can be looked at from two different perspectives and so explained in two different ways.

Do you remember Joseph, the jumped-up, coat-wearing dreamer? His eleven brothers got so sick of him that they decided to leave him in a pit to die. At least that was Plan A. When they caught sight of a bunch of potential investors, loaded with cash, they had a quick rethink and came up with a Plan B. They realised they could achieve their original aim (getting rid of Joseph) and make a quick buck at the same time, if they sold him as a slave.

It was disgraceful behaviour – just inexcusable. It was compounded by a clever cover-up: they fabricated evidence of Joseph's death by wild animals to deceive their Dad. The whole thing was a shameful incident that would come back to haunt them.

When they're unexpectedly reunited in Egypt, years later, it's no surprise that Joseph would say to them 'You meant evil against me...' (Gen. 50:20). That much is obvious. They wanted Joseph out of their lives forever. What might be more of a surprise is the follow-up. 'You meant evil against me, but God meant it for good, to bring it about that many people should be kept alive, as they are today.' It's a bit ironic: in God's plans, Joseph was the ticket to survival – when famine came – for the very brothers who'd tried to kill him. Get your mind around that!

There's no doubt that Joseph's exit from his family was a result of his brothers' wicked plans. But there's equally no doubt that – in another sense – it was God himself organising that exit.

The Joseph story is an example of a 'happy ending'. Everyone lives happily ever after the event in question. But sometimes it's not like that.

The death of King Saul paved the way for the great King David finally to become the universally recognised King of

Israel. Great for Israel – and David; not so much, perhaps, for King Saul.

But how did Saul die? It was a heat-of-the-moment decision. He'd gone into battle with the Philistines before, but this time they were just invincible. Israel was just no match for them that day. They'd already killed Saul's sons, including Jonathan, in the fray. And when Saul himself was wounded by an arrow, he realised that his number was up. Any moment now these barbarians would scoop him up. And when they did, one thing was for sure: his death would not be quick. They would play with him, humiliate him and most likely torture him.

He didn't need much time to think about it. Assisted suicide these days is usually a fairly clinical affair. On Saul's battlefield it was a bit more earthy. He had no painless injections to hand. No doctor in a white coat or bed to lie on. He just had a friend with a sword standing next to him. 'Do it', he said. When the man refused, Saul summoned up the strength to do it himself: 'Saul took his own sword and fell upon it' (1 Chron. 10:4).

Who was responsible for Saul's death? Clearly, Saul himself!

And yet just a few verses later, by way of a conclusion to the story, another perspective is offered: 'So Saul died for his breach of faith. He broke faith with the Lord in that he did not keep the command of the Lord, and also consulted a medium, seeking guidance. He did not seek guidance from the Lord. Therefore the Lord put him to death...'

Saul's suicide, then, came about as a spontaneous decision from the man himself: an act of personal self-interest. But at the very same time, it was explicitly and deliberately brought about by God: an act of judgement.

Once again, then, we see God and human beings at work – in different ways – in one and the same event.

There are any number of occasions where we could find a similar pattern: one event having both a God-explanation and a person-explanation.

By far the most notorious, though, is another death. But not just any death. I'm talking about the death of God's own son. Trying to pin the blame for this disgraceful act is not an easy job. There are just so many potential culprits. There's Judas who turned on his master. There's the crowd who shouted out 'Crucify him!' There's Pontius Pilate, who was too cowardly to put his foot down. There's the centurion who oversaw the crucifixion. There's even us – those whose sins were being punished there.

In the days following the ascension, the apostle Peter points the finger of blame squarely on his fellow Israelites. Jesus is the one 'whom you crucified', he tells the people of Israel on the day of Pentecost (Acts 2:36). 'You delivered over and denied [Jesus] in the presence of Pilate', he says to the crowd gathered in Solomon's portico. 'You denied the Holy and Righteous One... You killed the author of life...' (Acts 3:13-15). Can you hear the force of all those 'you's? There's no doubting who is responsible for this outrage.

But in almost the very same breath, Peter has no problem with explaining that ultimately God was behind what they were doing. 'What God foretold by the mouth of all the prophets, that his Christ would suffer, *he* thus fulfilled' (Acts 3:18). The various human culprits, he says in prayer to God, were 'gathered together against your holy servant Jesus... to do whatever *your* hand and *your* plan had predestined to take place' (Acts 4:27-28).

Were these events – the captivity of Joseph, the death of Saul, the crucifixion of Jesus – human actions or divine? The answer is: both! And the same is true of all those much less dramatic events which don't get the same level of explanation.

There are questions here about God's exact relationship with suffering and evil – and we'll come to that in chapter 3. But the point here is that while human beings are held responsible for their actions, that doesn't mean God isn't ultimately behind them – and vice versa. Every event has (at least) two explanations. 'The heart of man plans his way, but the Lord establishes his steps' (Prov. 16:9). Our actions are the normal ways that God achieves his purposes.

This might be the cause of a lot of head-scratching. It certainly does leave a few questions unanswered! But it also ought to be the cause of great encouragement to us when it comes to decision-making. You might have read what I said earlier about God's plan-will and – at least inwardly – thrown your arms up in the air.

'Isn't that just fatalism?' you might have asked. 'If God's already decided every detail of my life, what's the point in me even thinking about it? Is there even any point in getting out of bed every morning? If I can't actually affect my own future, why not just go with the flow and see where I end up!'

A moment's thought will help us to realise that what those questions suggest doesn't actually follow. The resolution not to think too much and the decision not to get out of bed are just as much considered choices as doing the more active alternative. Even if we did live in a world of fatalism, inactivity is not a logical response!

But we don't live in that world. What we've seen in this section is that God works out his good and wise plans *in and through* normal human thought-processes and behaviour. The fact that God plans and works doesn't mean we don't have to. It means quite the opposite.

If I go for a walk with my kids, it's me deciding where we're going. But they still have to burn up the energy, put one foot in front of the other, dodge the puddles and so on. And so it is with our heavenly Father's will and ours. If you ever need a sense of the significance of your life, think about this: every single thing you think, say or do – even the tiniest, most trivial detail, even the things you get wrong – is contributing to God's will being worked out in the world.

So much for the theory of God's will and how we fit into it. But what does all this mean for the connection between God and suffering?

Unshrinking God
in Suffering

The Christmas tree said it all. There it stood at the focus of the room. But it was a jarring sight. It stood askew, irritatingly angled off the vertical, like a miniature tower of Pisa. It seemed to sum up the past year for the family that sat around it. Nothing had gone right.

Opposite Bill sat his sister Jane. It was Jane's news which had rocked the family at the very beginning of the year. Yes, January 1st was the day her husband had made the announcement. It was inspired, apparently, by his new year's resolution of honesty and 'coming clean'. He was simply no longer in love with her, he said, and to live with her any longer would be to live a lie. And off he went. They had been married for less than three years.

Jane was heartbroken but worse was to come. The months that followed brought with them a series of aftershocks. The first discovery was that Jane was pregnant. News which should have brought joy to the hearts of a happy couple now left a prospective single parent anxious and confused. Then, instead of the reaction she had hoped for from her husband when she gave him the news, she was confronted with a further revelation. Despite his protestations, it transpired there had in fact been somebody else and he was now being public and permanent about this new relationship. Shortly afterwards, still reeling from this knock-out blow, Jane went for a routine scan and came home digesting something rather less than routine. The scan had picked up abnormalities in the foetus and – after exhaustive and exhausting further investigation – she was told it was unlikely the baby would live for long. In the end, 'not long' turned out to be just five days.

What had his sister done to deserve all this? Of all the people he knew, Jane was the one who had set the pace for those around her when it came to loving God and living for him.

Next to Jane sat Dad – even more taciturn than usual. He had barely uttered a syllable all evening.

Dad had known periods of melancholy before, but the experience of being laid off from work four months ago seemed to have triggered a complete emotional breakdown. He wasn't really surprised at being made redundant. As he went through the humiliating experience of reapplying for his own job, he was realistic enough to understand the game. Cutbacks had to be made. And despite his thirty years of service, the company just didn't deem him to be worth the premium his age and salary grade demanded. So after going through the steps of the required procedural dance, the company had bidden him a polite and financially generous, but nonetheless personally devastating, farewell.

And now, he could barely get out of bed in the morning. He would speak of living life entirely in shades of grey rather than in colour. He was aware of what a dark cloud he was in the house, how sapping his presence was, but the guilt he felt simply compounded his gloom. His self-confidence was shattered. His sleeping was fitful. Prayer was all but impossible. He found himself anxious about even the most trivial things. The medication he'd been prescribed had done no more to help than the well-intentioned pieces of advice from old friends.

Could God really be in this? Surely not! It was inconceivable that God would let a child of his experience suffer such deep distress.

Chris was next. Chris shouldn't be here at all, Bill remembered. He should be in Tanzania. But here he was, all six foot three of him. A gentle giant: a soft and kind heart inside a massive frame. This was supposed to be Chris's 'gap' year before university. Wanting to use his time to express God's love in practical action, he'd signed up with a community development organisation, and had jetted off to Africa in September for ten months. But just eight days into his project, as his team were dismantling an old structure to install some sewage facilities, a large block of concrete had fallen onto his forearm. It was wedged in such a way that it took over an hour for his fellow team-members to release him, by which time there was nothing that could be done to save his right hand. It was amputated at a local clinic.

That was the end of Chris's long-planned relief work. And of course it had put his plans for university and career in jeopardy. Even worse (for the moment), he was plagued by bursts of phantom pain. They were frequent and intense. His nerve system simply didn't get that his hand wasn't there. Chris could endure these episodes silently now – the only giveaway was his sharp breathing and his tightened and contorted face – but Bill knew he was in agony.

This simply could not be God's plan, Bill concluded. Maybe God had let it happen, but if so, it must have been only with the greatest reluctance.

And he hadn't even got to Mum yet – with her draining care for Grandad and his Alzheimers, and the distress of seeing her youngest son, Bill's brother Dave, walk away from the faith and in fact make a mess of life in just about every department imaginable.

Such troubles – and on so many sides! Perhaps, Bill wondered, it wasn't simply that God passively allowed such things to happen. Might it not be that God – rather than simply standing back and not intervening – had somehow been outflanked in the case of his family. Could there be spiritual forces in play here that were too powerful even for God?

After all, surely God wouldn't actually want Chris to lose a limb or Dad to plumb the depths of depression? But if he didn't – and they came to pass all the same – didn't that mean that God wasn't actually in control? Perhaps the devil or his minions were indeed running the show after all: Satan saw the good that Chris was doing in Africa and decided to bring it to a halt by causing that accident.

Or was it that God could intervene if he wanted to, but for some reason – perhaps to preserve human free will – he had stepped back and limited his own power to help? So Mum couldn't have been spared the pain of having a black sheep among her children, because Dave needed to have the option himself of walking away from the family. And God couldn't have kept Jane's marriage going without stripping her husband of his freedom to determine his own life.

These were all questions that needed pondering. And they were questions that mattered. They mattered because Bill needed to know what to say to his family. He needed to know how to help them find a pathway through their pain. He had seen enough to know that when people say the wrong thing – however well-intentioned they may be

– it can cause them real spiritual harm. He didn't want to make that mistake. And he needed to know how to pray for his family. And more than that, he needed to know how to react himself, should the coming year see him experience some form of serious trauma himself.

There was no doubt about it. How to think about God's relationship with suffering mattered enormously!

'Life is an onion. You peel it off, layer by layer, until you find there is nothing left of it – except tears in your eyes'.

Yes, I know. It's a pretty bleak perspective on life. But most of us know what the guy behind this quote was getting at. In fact, we might even find ourselves thinking along similar lines at one time or another. Live long enough and you will experience real pain first-hand. And even if you don't live that long, your early departure will most likely cause someone else to experience it because of you.

We thought about a few different forms of suffering back in chapter 1: disease, physical injury, relationship breakdown, unemployment, mental illness, infertility, bereavement, guilt. Those instances I gave were not crea-tions of my imagination. Those members of Bill's family are real people – albeit with the details mixed up a bit – that I've tried to help pastorally in the course of my ministry. The list could go on. I've sat down with people struggling with their sexuality, people struggling with eating disorders, people struggling with their personal finances, people struggling with their singleness, people struggling with relationships in their families or in the workplace or in their church, people struggling with sleep-deprivation, people struggling with the temptations of their own sinful selves.

The point is: real people struggle. And don't we know it?

But why does it have to be this way? How come there is all this suffering in the world?

WHY IS THERE SUFFERING?

Here's one answer to the question of suffering.

> Why is there all the suffering? Well it's like this. God wanted us to be able to decide how to live. Obviously. Otherwise we wouldn't really be human, would we? We'd just be robots. We needed to be able to make up our minds about whether to follow him or not and whether to do good or bad. So he gave us free will. Unfortunately, we took that free will and made bad decisions. We mucked up. Maybe he knew we would. Maybe he didn't. But either way, he left it up to us and we blew it. We started wrecking the place, and now look where we are...

Have you ever heard someone tackle the question in that way? Perhaps you've given that kind of answer yourself. I certainly have.

But if that's the tack you intend to take, I have one piece of advice. Change the subject quickly as soon as you've finished. Or else run away. Why? Because if you let the person you're speaking to think too much about what you've just said, you might find yourself in deep water. Here's where the conversation goes if you give them time to think about what you've just said.

> You're kidding! So God is so uninterested in the future of the human race that he just lets us go our own way? He knows full well the most cataclysmic event imaginable is about to happen to humanity. And he just sits back and

says: 'Well, if it's what they want!' Good job my parents didn't take that approach when I wandered out into the middle of the street as a five-year-old. What sort of a loving God would treat his creation like that?

What's that you say? He *didn't* know what was going to happen? OK, so now you're telling me that God is blind rather than just uncaring? He didn't know how things would turn out? That's meant to make me feel better? God designed us so that we might or might not self-destruct, then got himself a front row seat in the arena of life just to see what would happen? He basically just rolled the dice – that's what you're telling me?

What's that? He couldn't stop us from creating havoc for ourselves, because that would interfere with our free will and our human dignity? Well, I appreciate my dignity – thank you. That's probably about as much of a God as I can cope with having around. But I hope you don't mind my saying: he's not really much of a God then, is he?! I mean, you're always telling me I should live my life for God, but to be honest, as far as I can see, I'm not sure this scaled-down 'God-lite' is really worth *anyone* living their life for.

So let me just check I've got this right. You're saying he either didn't *care* enough to step in, or he didn't *know* what was going to happen, or – even if he did – he *couldn't help* anyway. You know what? I think I've already got a God like that. He's called Santa Claus.

Christians have always struggled to give a good answer for why there is suffering in the world. It's the big question that's thrown at us time and again. The so-called 'free-will defence' outlined above is a traditional and fairly common approach to answering the question. It's prompted by the desire to let God off the hook for all the pain.

But there are two big problems with it. The first is that – as we've seen – it doesn't succeed very well in letting God off the hook. That's got to be a pretty serious drawback. The second, though, is even more of a killer. It's that, quite frankly, God doesn't *want* to be let off the hook for the presence of suffering in the world!

Now that might come as a bit of a shock. But the Bible is 100 per cent clear on this. God is not behind only the good things in the world. He's also behind the hardships we go through.

GOD IS BEHIND THE PAIN TOO

Have a look at some of the ways the Bible describes the connection between God and suffering.

> 'Is it not from the mouth of the Most High that good and bad come?' (Lam. 3:38)

> 'I form light and create darkness, I make well-being and create calamity, I am the LORD who does all these things.' (Isa. 45:7)

> 'In the day of prosperity be joyful, and in the day of adversity consider: God has made the one as well as the other...' (Eccles. 7:14)

I know. This is eyebrow-raising stuff. It's strong medicine. It may be hard to swallow for many of us. We tend to thank God for the good things, because he was obviously behind them. But when life gets hard, we talk and act as though God were looking the other way. But the God of the Bible is a Big God – so big that he's behind *everything* that happens.

There are no exceptions.

No exceptions? Really? What about birth defects?

'Who has made man's mouth? Who makes him mute, or deaf, or seeing, or blind? Is it not I, the Lord?' (Exod. 4:11)

And financial woes?

'The Lord makes poor and makes rich; he brings low and he exalts.' (1 Sam. 2:7)

Droughts?

'I also withheld rain from you when there were yet three months to the harvest... and the field on which it did not rain would wither.' (Amos 4:7)

Surely not chronic medical conditions?

... a thorn was given me in the flesh... Three times I pleaded with the Lord about this, that it should leave me. (2 Cor. 12:7-8)

And infertility?

The LORD had closed her womb. (1 Sam. 1:5)

How about things that have been done to us by other people?

'And I will stir up Egyptians against Egyptians, and they will fight, each against another ...' (Isa. 19:2)

Floods and extreme weather events?

'He loads the thick cloud with moisture; the clouds scatter his lightning. They turn round and round by his guidance, to accomplish all that he commands them on the face of the habitable world.' (Job 37:11-12)

We could go on, but you get the point. As we read the Bible, we don't find God washing his hands of the troubles of the world. He doesn't say 'Not my fault'. Quite the reverse. He takes responsibility. He's quite clear that these things would not happen but for his decision.

Yes, these phenomena can be explained on one level by doctors, economists, meteorologists, psychologists and others. And on one level, their explanations are fine. But there is another, 'higher' level explanation for these things. Ultimately, troubling as it may be for us at first, these things happen because God has decided that they should happen.

Now, it's not quite that simple. If you read the Bible carefully and sensitively, you'll notice that there are occasionally subtle differences between the way God stands behind 'good' things and 'bad'. He stands *slightly* further back from the bad. For example, in Romans 9, those God has decided he will have mercy on are described as those 'whom he prepared in advance for glory' (Rom. 9:23, NIV). Whereas, in the previous verse, those he didn't decide to have mercy on are simply those 'prepared for destruction'. Did you spot the difference. God is not mentioned the second time. That's not to say God isn't in the mix. It's just that he doesn't actually *mention* it.

It's the same when Paul talks about his own experience. There's a similarly impersonal comment: 'there was given me a thorn in my flesh' (2 Cor. 12:7, NASB).

Like I said, subtle. But there are a number of little hints like that in the Bible. God doesn't stand behind the bad in exactly the same way as he stands behind the good.

But as we've seen, he still does stand behind them!

And of course that begs the question: why? Why would he do that? These are real people's lives he's messing with.

What could possibly bring a good, holy and loving God to bring pain and misery to those he's made in his own image?

One thing that has to be said at the outset is that we can only speak in generalities here. The Bible provides us with a number of things which God sets out to achieve through putting various particular individuals through times of suffering. What we *don't* get is a custom-made, fully personalised commentary on what God is seeking to do through the particular circumstances *you and I* (and our loved ones) are currently facing.

We'll come to questions of how we might respond personally to suffering later. For now, though, let's think about the three things that God is on record as using suffering to achieve.

MAKING US MORE LIKE JESUS

God uses suffering, in the first place, to shape his children. He has a clear objective for us and that is to make us more like his son Jesus. And he will use everything at his disposal to achieve that aim: his word, the example of fellow Christians, answers to prayer, material blessings, the encouragements and rebukes of others, and so on.

But Christian people of every generation have found that the times when they grew in their discipleship the most were not the easy times but the hard ones. The experience of pain is another – and perhaps the most effective – tool used by God to make us more like his son Jesus.

Have a read of these couple of verses.

> I walked a mile with pleasure,
> She chattered all the way,
> But left me none the wiser
> For all she had to say.

I walked a mile with sorrow
And never a word said she,
But oh the things I learned from her,
When sorrow walked with me.

Can you identify with that in your experience? For most of us, it will take only a moment's thought to realise the truth of this. Seasons of hardship tend to be seasons of growth. But what kind of growth are we talking about?

For one thing, God uses pain to grow our *humility*. Nobody likes people who are proud and full of themselves. But deep down, we know that there's often a good bit of that in each of us, especially when it comes to our relationship with God. Making us feel self-sufficient is one of sin's primary tactics to convincing us we don't need God all that much. So we have a natural tendency to big ourselves up in our own eyes. And sometimes the only thing that will bring us down to size is real personal suffering.

The book of 2 Corinthians is Paul's most personal and self-revealing letter. It's where we find him wearing his heart on his sleeve more than anywhere else. And he is pretty candid about how hard life has been for him. More than once he's thought it was curtains for him. But as he looks back on those horrendous times, he has a God-given perspective on what was going on behind the scenes.

We do not want you to be ignorant, brothers, of the affliction we experience in Asia. For we were so utterly burdened beyond our strength that we despaired of life itself. Indeed, we felt that we had received the sentence of death. But **that was to make us rely not on ourselves but on God** who raises the dead. (2 Cor. 1:8-9)

Even Paul, then, needed a few corners being knocked off him so as to keep looking to God. The experiences of life he went through were designed by God to nurture, deepen his trust and dependence on his heavenly father.

But even that wasn't enough. Later in the letter we learn that Paul's health had also come under attack. We don't know the details, but it seems he had some kind of chronic illness or disability. And once again, his God-given perspective on this was that it was itself God-given.

> ... A thorn was given me in the flesh, a messenger of Satan to harass me, to keep me from becoming conceited. Three times I pleaded with the Lord about this, that it should leave me. But he said to me, 'My grace is sufficient for you, for my power is made perfect in weakness.' (2 Cor. 12:7-9)

Now don't miss the point here. The point is not simply that God is still there even when things are tough. It's much more than that. It's that we *need* the experience of suffering to avoid becoming full of ourselves, to remember to keep looking to him for strength and to keep seeing God for the mind-blowingly powerful God that he is. And that perspective is so important for us to hang on to that – even though he loves us – God is prepared to put us through hard times to make sure we keep hold of it.

But humility is not the only area we need to grow in. God also uses pain to grow our *holiness*. Most of us have some idea how far we have to go in this area. We know we're well short of the finished article. But none of us takes it anything like as seriously as we should, or indeed as God does. God is determined to make us worthy of our title 'sons of God'.

The Christians addressed in the New Testament's Letter to the Hebrews had gone through appalling hardship. They'd been taunted and discriminated against. Some of them had lost their houses. Others were imprisoned. It was a really rough road they'd been walking. And it would have been the easiest and most obvious thing in the world to blame their persecutors for their troubles.

But the writer points the finger in a different direction – at God himself. And, more than that, he's explicit about what God is up to.

> It is for discipline that you have to endure. God is treating you as sons. For what son is there whom his father does not discipline? If you are left without discipline, in which all have participated, then you are illegitimate children and not sons. Besides this, we have had earthly fathers who disciplined us and we respected them. Shall we not much more be subject to the Father of spirits and live? For they disciplined us for a short time as it seemed best to them, but he disciplines us for our good, that we may share his holiness. For the moment of discipline seems painful rather than pleasant, but later it yields the peaceful fruit of righteousness to those who have been trained by it. (Heb. 12:7-11)

When Michelangelo began work on his famous sculpture of David, his raw material was not promising. The block of marble from which he worked had already been rejected by Donatello. It had too many imperfections. But Michelangelo saw what he could make of it. So he set to work. For two years he hammered and chipped away with his chisel. And on 25 January 1504 the veil was dropped to reveal a sculpture that would prove to take the breath away from millions of viewers. But it could not have been done without the hard cutting edge of that chisel.

It's the same with God's work on us. When life is painful, it is not God punishing us for some particular sin we have committed. Rather it is God sculpting us into the spiritual works of art he plans to make of us. Suffering is God's way of refining us. It is the rough track along which our divine life-chauffeur drives us to get us to our destination of Christ-like character. It is the painful regime our personal trainer takes us through to build up our spiritual muscle. It is the tough love with which our heavenly father raises children who are worthy of the family name.

Finally, suffering is also God's way of growing us in *hope*. Twenty-first century life in the West is so comfortable for so many in many ways we have lost the need – perhaps even the ability – to look forward. African slaves working in the cotton fields of the American south hadn't lost it. They got through each day by reminding each other of future deliverance in the songs they sang. 'Swing low, sweet chariot', they chanted, 'Comin' for to carry me home'.

Suffering Christian believers in every generation have had their focus thrown forward in the same way. Many could have written the words of Theodore Cuyler: 'To my weak vision, dimmed with tears, the cloud is exceeding dark, but through it stream some rays from the infinite love that fills the Throne with an exceeding and eternal brightness of glory'. In living by faith as well as experience, we find we're better able and indeed more inclined to celebrate the truth of Psalm 30:5. 'Weeping may tarry for the night, but joy comes in the morning.'

Well, that's one thing suffering does for us: it makes us more like Jesus – it's an opportunity to grow our humility, our holiness and our hope.

DRAWING PEOPLE TO JESUS
The second is that our suffering actually has a crucial part to play in God's purposes for drawing people to Jesus. You may have heard that C.S. Lewis quote about suffering.

'God whispers to us in our pleasures, he speaks to us in our conscience, but he shouts to us in our pain. [Pain] is God's megaphone to rouse a deaf world.'

I think that's the experience of many people. When life is going well, they feel invincible, care-free, self-assured. It takes things going wrong in their lives to make them realise just how fragile life is and how superficial their values and ambitions have been to this point. Suffering is the acid which dissolves some of that armour of invincibility and makes us open to the atmosphere in the world beyond ourselves.

I still remember the day I met a terrorist. The 'Shining Path' was a fearsome organisation. They murdered tens of thousands of people back in the 1980s and '90s in Peru. And here I was, high up in the Peruvian Andes, talking to one of them. But the place where I met him was not a training camp or even a prison. It was a church. It had taken the deaths of his entire family in government reprisals for the terrorism to bring him to his senses and make him realise the folly of his path. His pain had led him to God.

That seems to have been how it was with the woman of Samaria (John 4:1-26). You don't get through five husbands in a Middle-Eastern culture without people raising eyebrows. In fact, they probably did a lot worse than raise eyebrows. But it was to her that Jesus chose to reveal himself.

And it's how it is time and again today. Real suffering is what it takes for many to wake up to the truth of God's claim upon their lives.

But actually, if you follow the contours of the Bible, you quickly realise there's much more to say than that.

For one thing, God uses suffering to embolden gospel-tellers. It functions as a motivation to us to get on and share the gospel. That's apparently what happened with Paul when he was in prison.

> And most of the brothers, having become confident in the Lord by my imprisonment, are much more bold to speak the word without fear. (Phil. 1:14)

In other words Paul suffering in prison was a spur to the evangelism of his fellow believers. The link is not spelt out for us, but it's not hard to see how Christian people might see someone being so fearless in his evangelism that he gets into trouble for it and starts thinking: 'Hey, when I look at him, I feel like I'm not really pulling my weight here! Maybe I should start taking this evangelism seriously instead of just talking about it!'

Twentieth-century China saw what is perhaps the most determined effort in history to stamp out Christianity. Missionaries were expelled. Meetings were banned. Known believers were persecuted. Pastors were imprisoned or even executed. But God's people didn't disappear. Far from it – they were spurred on in their witness to Jesus! And so it was that – between 1949 (when the Communist Party came to power and began to stamp down on Christianity) and today, the number of Christians in China has actually grown – and grown explosively. One estimate is that they have increased from 5 million to 80 million in that period.

God uses suffering to embolden the gospel-tellers.

Then secondly, God uses suffering to create gospel opportunities. The classic example of this is in the book of Acts, when after the stoning of Stephen, the authorities decided to try to nip this Christian movement in the bud.

> And there arose on that day a great persecution against the church in Jerusalem, and they were all scattered throughout the regions of Judea and Samaria, except the apostles. (Acts 8:1)

Given how fragile the Christian movement was, we might expect that this would spell the end. But it didn't. In God's purposes, relocating those Christians just meant multiplying the places where the gospel could be told.

So verse 4: 'Now those who were scattered went about preaching the word.'

I wonder how many times something like that has been repeated through Christian history on all sorts of scales. Jo gets sick and goes to hospital. Starts chatting to the person in the next bed, and that person is converted and becomes a missionary. Bill gets laid off at work and takes up running to give himself some routine through the months of unemployment that follow. Finds himself going out regularly with someone in the same boat who's deeply impressed with Bill's attitude of trust in God. 'I want what you've got', he says one day and commits his life to Christ, and becomes a tireless evangelist among his colleagues when he returns to work. Any number of times something like that must have happened. Maybe that will be what happens through *our* suffering, when that time comes.

Third, God uses suffering to enable people to hear and respond to the gospel.

That prospect seems to have been what kept Paul going at times in his ministry. 'If we are afflicted [he wrote to the Corinthians], it is for your salvation.' (2 Cor. 1:5-6) Or to Timothy: 'Remember Jesus Christ, risen from the dead, the offspring of David, as preached in my gospel, for which I am suffering, bound with chains as a criminal. But the word of God is not bound! Therefore I endure everything for the sake of the elect, that they also may obtain the salvation that is in Christ Jesus with eternal glory (2 Tim. 2:8-10).

Now what's going on here? Well, there's a very interesting comment Paul makes in Colossians 1. 'Now I rejoice in my sufferings for your sake, and in my flesh I am filling up what is lacking in Christ's afflictions for the sake of his body, that is, the church.' (Col. 1:24)

What can he mean there? Is he saying Christ didn't suffer quite enough to accomplish salvation? No, not at all. Christ's suffering was complete and perfect. He did everything that was needed to achieve our salvation and of all the people who would ever come to him. What was 'lacking in Christ's afflictions' wasn't anything related to *accomplishing* salvation. It was all to do with *communicating* that salvation. Taking the good news of Jesus to the world is itself an inherently painful task. It brings with it the risk of rejection, mockery, persecution, or possibly even imprisonment and death.

But the painful lifestyle of the person who is serious about evangelism is yet another picture of how God uses suffering to advance his gospel. If we recognise that this may well be what God is intending when we go through hard times, we will find it a wonderful comfort. The truth will dawn on us: we're not suffering for nothing! One day when we turn up to the pearly gates there may be somebody, maybe many people, who come up to us and say 'thank you'. Had we not faced the pain we faced, they would not be in the kingdom.

BRINGING GLORY TO JESUS
Finally, **God uses suffering to achieve glory for his Son, the Lord Jesus Christ.** It's an obvious point, but a point worth making nevertheless: were it not for the possibility of suffering in the world, there would be no cross. And if there were no cross, if Jesus were not humiliated and beaten and crucified, then the scene of Revelation 5 could never happen.

Here are the twenty-four elders, falling down before the Lamb, and here are their words...

And they sang a new song, saying,

'Worthy are you to take the scroll and to open its seals, for you were slain, and by your blood you ransomed people for God from every tribe and language and people and nation, and you have made them a kingdom and priests to our God, and they shall reign on the earth.'

Then I looked, and I heard around the throne and the living creatures and the elders the voice of many angels, numbering myriads of myriads and thousands of thousands, saying with a loud voice, 'Worthy is the Lamb who was slain, to receive power and wealth and wisdom and might and honour and glory and blessing!' (Rev. 5:9-12)

Jesus is not acknowledged as simply the King. No, he will forever be 'the Lamb who was slain'. Those nails may have disfigured his flesh, but at the same time they have made him more beautiful, more celebrated, more glorious – for all eternity.

So what's the upshot of all this? It's that we may not know all that God is doing when life gets hard for us or the people we love. But we do have full confidence that he does. God knows *exactly* what he's doing by allowing suffering in the world.

RESPONDING TO SUFFERING

In this chapter, we've seen how recognising that God remains in the driving seat – even when the road is a painful one – allows us to be better attuned to just what God may be achieving in suffering. But it wouldn't be right to close without coming down to earth a bit. So here are just nine brief pointers in how we might respond to suffering.

How to Respond to Pain

1. Speak to God openly about your suffering. You may find the Psalms useful to articulate some of the things you feel. He is your heavenly Father and loves to hear the voice of his children. 'Hear my cry, O Lord; listen to my prayer. From the ends of the earth I call to you, I call as my heart grows faint...' (Ps. 61:1-2, NIV). Say how you feel, and ask for deliverance by all means, but pray too that he would accomplish his purposes through your pain.

2. Ask God to give you the stamina and patience you need to bear your suffering well. He promised the apostle Paul, 'My grace is sufficient for you' (2 Cor. 12:9). Claim that promise for yourself.

3. Invite others to help you in your pain. They may not know the right thing to say, but recognise their good intentions. They may offer to help practically; accept their help with grace. This is what families do. 'Carry each other's burdens, and in this way you will fulfil the law of Christ' (Gal. 6:2, NIV).

4. Give thanks for what God will achieve in you through this pain you are experiencing – both the things you know about (e.g. refining your faith 'so that it may be proved genuine', 1 Pet. 1:7, NIV) and the things you don't. Everyone experiences suffering, to a degree. The believer, though, has the comfort that it is not meaningless; it is accomplishing God's purposes.

5. Don't give in to fear. God is your loving heavenly Father who is totally committed to finishing the good work he has begun in you. Nothing can take away your eternal security. He cares. 'Indeed the very hairs on your head are all numbered. Don't be afraid. You are worth more than many sparrows' (Luke 12:7, NIV).

6. Focus your dependence on God, and so consciously draw the benefit from your pain. Acknowledge that God has allowed you to go through this out of his *love* for you (not his displeasure), because he wants to deepen your dependence on him as opposed to the comforts you have lost. 'This happened that we might not rely on ourselves but on God, who raises the dead' (2 Cor. 1:9, NIV).

---

7. If your suffering has been caused by a person, or people, guard your heart against feelings of hatred or revenge. 'Bless those who persecute you... do not repay evil with evil... overcome evil with good' (Rom. 12:14-21, NIV).

8. Don't distance yourself from God's word. You need to be listening to your heavenly father now more than ever. In fact in your suffering, you will see things in his word you have never seen before ('Your word is a lamp to my feet, and a light to my path', Ps. 119:105, NIV).

9. Keep sharing your life with others. You may instinctively be tempted to turn inwards, but remember: at this point of obvious weakness, your life and words may have more power to commend the gospel to unbelievers, or to encourage believers, than at any other time of your life. Remember Paul's experience: 'what has happened to me has really served to advance the gospel... Because of my chains, most of the brothers in the Lord have been encouraged to speak the word of God more courageously and fearlessly' (Phil. 1:12:-14, NIV).

10. Look forward. Whatever this life holds, 'an inheritance that can never perish, spoil or fade' is being 'kept in heaven for you'; what's more, you yourself are being spiritually preserved, 'shielded by God's power', for it (1 Pet. 1:4-5, NIV).

Our experience of pain is perhaps the most life-impacting and gut-wrenching issue to work through in the light of a God who is actively working out his purposes in the world.

But it's not the only such issue. If God really is in control, where does that leave – for example – our efforts to spread the gospel?

Unshrinking God
in Evangelism

It was just ten days now before the start of the church mission week. A whole array of events and activities designed to reach out to the community around church. And Emily was on the Planning Team.

She was there mainly because of her near-inability to say no to anyone. The cry had gone up that somebody 'good at organising things' was needed for the team. Emily's name was mentioned. And before she knew it, the mission week was filling her inbox with more messages than every other part of her life put together.

It was exciting, of course, but a big part of her would be relieved when it was all over. It wasn't so much the workload. It was more the angst, and particularly the issues that had started swirling through her head since a tricky team meeting just a month ago.

The programme was all set. The publicity was about to go out. It was mainly just practical details and niggles that needed to be sorted out. And much of it had been. The meeting was about to come to an end. 'Any other business?' asked the lady chairing the team in a way that indicated she clearly wasn't expecting a positive answer.

And then out it came. 'Don't you think we should pray a bit more?' Emily had said. 'I mean we've spent almost two hours planning things and – what – three minutes praying? I mean, nothing good is going to happen with this mission week unless God does it, right?' Everyone looked at Emily. Emily went bright red. What was she doing, speaking like that? She didn't realise she'd even had this concern before she heard herself blurting it out!

Of course they decided to close with a few minutes prayer: 'Good idea, Emily', someone had said. But the coming days saw her articulate more and more worries about what they were really doing and why.

The matter she raised was the start. She recalled just how much planning had gone into the week's programme. Hundreds of hours, maybe thousands. Everything had been thought of. The right venues (very classy!), the right mix of events (something for everyone), the right hosts (confident, good-looking and articulate), the right speakers (full of passion) the right publicity (a whole web campaign as well as the glossy flyers), the right ambience (relaxed and welcoming), the right music (very professional), the right entertainment content (laughter would flow) – everything. And all to make it bring members of the audience a step closer to the Kingdom of God.

But could you really grease somebody's slide into the kingdom like this? Wasn't conversion the work of the Holy Spirit, not the work of slick entertainers and musicians? Or was she wrong about this? Maybe you could impress somebody – or indeed argue them – into the kingdom.

That said, the aim of this mission week didn't really seem to be about the kingdom anyway. It was more about the church. 'They've got to belong before they'll believe', someone had said in a sage voice, to a murmur of approval from the rest of the team. Emily had said nothing on that occasion, but that hadn't stopped her worrying.

It felt like the strategy was to ease them into the church, and then sit back as – bit by bit – they became so comfortable with their new friends that they just kind of gently – and painlessly, and almost without noticing – slipped into salvation. It didn't seem much like how it was done in the Book of Acts! Didn't Peter and Paul confront people with the gospel and challenge them to respond to it? This whole mission week programme felt just a bit – well, sneaky! All a bit human. She was trying to avoid saying – even to herself – the word 'manipulative'.

How much of all this human activity and planning was needed to bring someone to faith?

But now Emily was on a roll. In the days that followed, her thoughts took a different direction.

Actually, she thought, why do we need to do anything at all? If God really elects his people, then surely they'll make it into the kingdom somehow, whatever we do. We could call off this whole mission week and it wouldn't make the slightest bit of difference! If God's already got his list of names, what chance do we have of adding or subtracting a single entry on it?!

What was the point of evangelism at all, when God's in control?

They call it the kiss of life, and it's not hard to see why. Every year thousands of people who have experienced heart failure are given CPR, often with dramatic results.
    And it doesn't get much more dramatic than the case of star footballer Fabrice Muamba. On 17 March 2012,

playing an FA Cup Match in front of tens of thousands at White Hart Lane in London, Muamba suddenly collapsed forty-three minutes into the game. He fell to the ground, spectators said, 'like a tree trunk'. His heart simply stopped beating and he collapsed unconscious.

At that moment, the statistical stopwatch started: like everyone else who experiences cardiac arrest, for every minute that went by before he was given help, his chances of survival were decreasing by 10 percent. Big picture? Nine out of every ten people who suffer cardiac arrest outside a hospital, as Muamba did, will not live.

But there was good news. Not only was there a full medical team on hand, but among the fans that day was consultant cardiologist Dr Andrew Deaner from the London Chest Hospital who was able to take control of the situation. CPR was started quickly – and professionally. The defibrillator was soon ready to go (Muamba was to receive a total of 4,500 Joules of electricity over fifteen shocks). And the ambulance was not far away.

Muamba's heart stopped for seventy-eight minutes that day. To all intents and purposes he was dead. But the kiss of life meant he lived another day.

Each and every time someone turns to Jesus for the first time, it's a death-to-life experience. There are no exceptions. It's the basic spiritual biography of every Christian. 'As for you, you were dead' says Paul in Ephesians 2:1. 'But', he goes on to tell us, we've now been made 'alive' (vv. 4-5, NIV).

So every one of us who's in God's kingdom has received the kiss of spiritual life. The only question is: who gave it to us? Our friend? Our pastor? Our parents? The visiting evangelist? The speaker at camp? The leader of our youth group?

It's natural to feel a sense of deep gratitude to the person who guided us into our friendship with Christ. They did a great work and things have changed for ever for us! But ultimately, it's not they who gave us the kiss of life. Here's a bit more of Ephesians 2:4-5.

> But God, being rich in mercy, because of the great love with which he loved us, even when we were dead in our trespasses, made us alive together with Christ.

God is the giver of spiritual life. When I turned to Jesus, it wasn't ultimately down to the persuasive powers of the man who laid it all out for me. And it wasn't down to the considered decision I made – even though that's probably how it felt at the time. It was down to God.

The Bible is 100 per cent clear on that. Again and again, we're told that the decision we made to start trusting Jesus was ultimately God's doing. Look at some of these verses.

> 'No one can come to me unless the Father who sent me draws him.' (John 6:44)

> 'God exalted him... to give repentance to Israel and forgiveness of sins. ...to the Gentiles also God has granted repentance that leads to life.' (Acts 5:31; 11:18)

> For by grace you have been saved through faith. And this is not your own doing; it is the gift of God. (Eph. 2:8)

> It has been granted to you that for the sake of Christ you should... believe in him... (Phil. 1:29)

You get the gist. However our spiritual story has been played out, the underlying reality is that it was God who wrote the script. It was God who picked me out – for reasons known only to himself – and did all that was needed to bring me into his kingdom. I could never have come to him off my own bat. None of us could. As unbelievers, we were blind – totally unable to see things as they are and recognise the truth. We were slaves to sin – lacking any freedom to seek out an alternative master. We were under the power of Satan and trapped in his kingdom. We were spiritually dead – incapable of administering any aid to ourselves. We needed God – working through his Son and his Spirit – to restore our sight, break our chains, get us out of Satan's realm and give us new life.

Fabrice Muamba was not simply offered *assistance* that day as he lay on the pitch. The medics didn't just hold out a helping hand and wait for him to respond having considered his options. Why not? Because he was out cold. He didn't have the capacity to accept a helping hand or say yes to the doctors. He was unconscious and as good as dead. He needed them to make the decisions and do what needed doing.

When we begin to grasp that the unbelievers we know – and once were ourselves – are in much the same position spiritually speaking, we'll understand why the initiative for our coming into God's kingdom *has* to come from God himself.

But that doesn't mean it's not hard to get our heads around. It's hard because it's a full-on, frontal assault on our autonomy. We thought we were calling the shots when it came to deciding for or against God. It seemed to us as though God was in the dock and we were in the jury. It was simply us considering the evidence for or against his existence and his claim on our lives. But now we learn it was the other way around! Our thought processes and choices were real and authentic, but on another level they were being guided by God himself.

That doesn't sit well with most of us. We might be willing to let God into the driving seat for the world as a whole, and maybe even some of our decision-making. But the decision we made to follow him? Surely that must be sacrosanct?! It seems not. So we need to ask God for humility and the ability to keep ourselves from kicking and screaming (or the spiritual equivalent) as the Bible cuts us down to size.

But there's something else that's hard. The Bible's teaching that it's ultimately God who gives the kiss of spiritual life is not just a blow to our *pride* (because we thought we could self-administer). It's potentially a source of confusion about our *role* – specifically, our role in evangelism. If it all comes down to God, if faith itself is his to give, where do all our efforts to communicate the gospel fit in?

William Carey, the eighteenth century cobbler-turned missionary, is sometimes described as the 'father of modern missions'. I'm not sure he'd have cared for the description. But if you were to look for the spark that lit the flame for the explosion of missionary activity over the last 200 years, Carey's writing and example is a serious contender.

But when it came to getting his contemporaries excited about the work of the gospel overseas, he had his work cut out. 'Young man', he was told when he floated the idea of starting a missionary society, 'Sit down. When God pleases to convert the heathen, he will do it without your aid or mine.'

Now that's what I call confusion about our role in evangelism! You know you've come off the rails when the place you get to is 'we shouldn't tell people about Jesus'.

So what does it mean for God to be king in the realm of evangelism? And how does it affect our approach?

GOD DETERMINES THE MESSAGE

First of all, it is God, not us, who determines the message we take to those around us.

Our tendency today is to associate life with freshness, creativity and innovation. But the Bible takes the opposite view when it comes to the gospel message. The only way to offer life to those around us is to leave the gospel we have inherited intact. No touching up. No remastering. No adaptation. Why? Because to modify God's gospel is not to bring life; it's to return to death.

The apostle Paul was the original gospel pioneer: far-sighted, entrepreneurial, energetic, brilliant, committed to crossing boundaries and breaking new ground with the message. If there was anyone in the first generation of Christians you'd expect to get creative with the gospel in some way, or indeed encourage others to bring it up to date, it would be him. But see how he speaks to the Christians in Corinth.

> Now I would remind you, brothers, of the gospel I preached to you, which you received, in which you stand, and by which you are being saved, if you hold fast to the word I preached to you – unless you believed in vain. For I delivered to you as of first importance what I also received: that Christ died for our sins in accordance with the Scriptures. (1 Cor. 15:1-3)

Did you spot the stress on continuity? Paul passed on what was passed to him – and he expects the Corinthians to do the same. The only way to salvation – to life! – was to maintain the gospel entirely unchanged. His role – and by implication the role of all who have heard and responded to the gospel message is to be 'servants of Christ and stewards of the mysteries of God' (1 Cor. 4:1-2). And as everyone knows, the primary job of a steward is to preserve and protect the thing that's been entrusted to him or her.

The message is not ours. It is the 'gospel of God' (Rom. 1:1). He thought of it. He enacted it. And he entrusted it to us for safe-keeping.

So our primary task in the work of the gospel is simply to preserve it! That may sound pretty straightforward, but the reality is many of us fall at this first hurdle. The desire to make the gospel 'relevant' has led to Christians around the world modifying it and so effectively robbing it of its saving power.

MAKING THE GOSPEL MORE RELEVANT?

Here are just three of the many altered gospels Christians have come up with over the past hundred years or so in order to make it engage more with the world around. You may have seen elements of all three still alive and well in ministries you've experienced!

1. THE SOCIAL GOSPEL

This gospel is about transforming social systems in the here and now. Jesus came to bring social and economic equality for all, to rid the world of poverty and oppression.

✓ Gets the basic plan right: Jesus did come to inaugurate God's kingdom.

✗ Gets the problem wrong: our biggest problem is not the effect of other peoples' sins but the effect of our own.

2. THE PROSPERITY GOSPEL

This gospel is about increasing the material comforts of believers in this world. Jesus came to make possible freedom from sickness and to make me financially better off.

✓ Gets God's favour right: he is committed to pouring his blessings out on his people.

✗ Gets the timing wrong: life this side of glory, the norm for Christians is as much pain as material blessing. The best is yet to come.

> **3. THE THERAPEUTIC GOSPEL**
>
> The gospel is about boosting my sense of personal fulfilment and happiness. Jesus came to make me feel loved, to raise my self-esteem and to offer a sense of purpose and significance to my life.
>
> ✓ Gets our response right: Spirit-given joy and confident hope are marks of the true believer.
>
> ✗ Gets the focus wrong: the gospel is not so much about improving my life as about rescuing me from death.

In practice, then, given the tendencies in Western Christianity today, the primary challenge to most of us will be to ask ourselves what we think the gospel message really is. Which one of the following is a bigger deal to us: the felt needs Jesus might meet in us or the spiritual needs he promises to meet? Which do we expect to experience: a life of the prosperity we'd all like or a life of the suffering Jesus modelled? What do we see Jesus doing at the cross: showing us how much we're worth to him or taking the punishment for our sin? Which is higher up our agenda: growing in intimacy with Jesus or putting sin to death?

It's not hard to figure out what people we know would like to hear as the gospel message and to give the spin we think will lead to an easy reception. The hard thing is to stick to God's unaltered gospel and trust that he'll do his work through it.

But actually this is good news. It means the pressure is off. We don't need, after all, to expend all that mental and emotional energy getting creative with the shape of the message. And that's handy, because we're going to need that energy for other things...

GOD COMMISSIONS THE MESSENGERS

A second way God's rule affects our evangelism is that he commissions his people as his messengers and ambassadors. He places the responsibility to speak squarely upon our shoulders. And that takes bringing the gospel to the world around us firmly out of the 'optional extra' box. No longer can we kid ourselves that evangelism is the 'rear parking camera' of the Christian life. It's more like the steering wheel.

Jesus was clear about this work.

> 'All authority in heaven and on earth has been given to me. Therefore go and make disciples of all nations, baptising them in the name of the Father and of the Son and of the Holy Spirit, and teaching them to obey everything I have commanded you...'. (Matt. 28:18-20, NIV)

It's an ongoing work, this work of disciple-making. It passes from generation to generation. Why? Because part of disciple-making, says Jesus, is passing on the commands of Jesus – including, presumably, this one! To be a disciple is to be a disciple-maker.

Paul was just as clear. Chapters 8 to 10 of 1 Corinthians is a long passage all about giving up personal rights for the benefit of others. It includes a long worked example of how this works out for Paul himself. 'I have become all things to all people', he says, 'so that by all possible means I might save some' (1 Cor. 9:22, NIV). The work of the gospel, in other words, is Paul's absolute priority that leads him to sacrifice the things he might otherwise feel entitled to. But, interestingly, he concludes the whole section with a summary application: 'For I am not seeking my own good but the good of many, so that they may be saved. Follow my example as I follow the example of Christ' (1 Cor. 10:33–11:1, NIV).

How much have you given up of what you feel entitled to, in order to see the work of the gospel go forward?

One way to know if the gospel has really gripped a believer is to see how much they prioritise passing it on. That's why Paul found such encouragement in what happened in and around Thessalonica. He saw the commitment of the believers there to spreading the gospel as a sure sign that they'd truly accepted it: '...you welcomed the message with the joy given by the Holy Spirit... The Lord's message rang out from you not only in Macedonia and Achaia – your faith in God has become known everywhere' (1 Thess. 1:6-8, NIV).

Of course there are always going to be some who have a particular aptitude towards getting alongside unbelievers and explaining the gospel to them in an effective and persuasive way. Some people have just 'got it'. It's their 'thing'. And that shouldn't be a surprise. The Bible talks about a specific 'gift' of evangelism (Eph. 4:11). So the fact that most of us find it a real struggle shouldn't make us feel like failures.

But remember: God's big plan is 'to bring all things in heaven and on earth together under one head, even Christ' (Eph. 1:10, NIV 1984). And the way he's chosen to do that is not by pressing some huge divine remote control so that everyone suddenly bows the knee. No, he's chosen to do it by employing people like you and me. He commissions *us* to be his ambassadors. He 'gave us the ministry of reconciliation...' (2 Cor. 5:18, NIV). *Our lives and our words* are the way his plan will be fulfilled.

GOD DECIDES THE STRATEGY

Does your church or the ministry you're involved in have a strategy for reaching the lost? A zippy website backed up by search engines ranking optimisation techniques? A programme of attractive events and appealing activities designed to ease people into the community? A training course to get people geared up for outreach? A survey-driven portfolio of ministries aimed at meeting the felt needs of local residents and from there provide gospel-sharing opportunities?

There may be place for any – or indeed all – of these things in preparing to reach unbelievers. But it's interesting how much simpler the New Testament strategy is. You could sum it up in just three words:

1. Love

> 'A new command I give you', said Jesus. 'Love one another. By this everyone will know that you are my disciples, if you love one another'. (John 13:34-35, NIV)

Here is the central prong of God's public relations campaign for the gospel. It's the visible love of a Christian community. You think you need to choose between a commitment to fellow believers and reaching unbelievers? Wrong! That's a human logic. The divine logic says: start with loving one another, let the world see that, and you'll be off on the right foot when you start explaining the gospel.

2. Live

As in: live a godly and attractive life. Here's the second prong of God's gospel-advertising campaign. It's his specific plan for marriages where one partner gets converted: '...if any of them [husbands] do not believe the word, they may be won over... when they see the purity and reverence of your lives' (1 Pet. 3:1-2, NIV). But it's more than that. It's his general plan for the whole community too. 'Live such good lives among the pagans that, though they accuse you of doing wrong, they may see your good deeds and glorify God on the day he visits us' (1 Pet. 2:12).

Again the divine logic goes in a different direction to human logic. Our instinct is to take the spotlight off our lives. After all, we're understandably embarrassed about the hypocrisy that will be on show. In fact many of us put a high value on our privacy. We'd rather keep people at arm's length. But God's approach is different. Work at your lives. Work at your godliness. Work at speaking and behaving in such a way that those around you want what you've got! Because then they'll listen to what you say.

Yes, you can bowl up to a random passer-by in the street and share the gospel. Of course you can. Don't let anyone tell you you've got to 'earn the right' or any such rubbish. You've *got* the right. Jesus said: 'All authority... has been given to me. Therefore go...!' That's all the 'right' we need. But the way God has set up the world, people listen better when they've got respect for the speaker.

3. Speak

I wonder if you've heard that little dictum of Francis of Assisi: 'Preach the gospel always; if necessary use words.' It's generally used to back up a kind of shrunk down, gospel-lite version of the Christian message (something along the lines of 'be nice to people'). But it's been doing the rounds in Bible-believing Christian circles over the past decade or two.

There are two problems with it. One, St Francis never actually said it. At least not as far as anyone's been able to find. (The reality is: someone in the 1990s decided that he'd said it and round it went. Hardly surprisingly. After all, it's a killer quote!)

And two, it's *always* necessary! Nobody's going to look at an act of kindness and think: 'Wow, that's beautiful. I should turn to Christ in faith and repentance, asking him to forgive me my sins on the basis of his death at the cross, and resolving to serve him as Lord for the rest of my life'. At least not if they (a) don't know the kind person was actually a Christian, (b) have never even heard of Jesus, sin or the cross, except as words for swearing with, advertising triple-chocolate deserts and describing what they do with their fingers when they want good luck, respectively or (c) haven't been taught the need to respond to the gospel. They need explanations. They need us to speak.

We must be prepared to speak.

We're to speak *faithfully* (making sure we're accurate in our summary of the gospel). 'For what I received I passed on to you as of first importance' (1 Cor. 15:3, NIV).

We're to speak *clearly* (working hard to make sure we're actually understood). 'Pray that I may proclaim it clearly, as I should', said Paul (Col. 4:4, NIV).

We're to speak courageously (being prepared to risk our own comfort and safety for the sake of the gospel). 'Now Lord, ...enable your servants to speak your word with great boldness' (Acts 4:29, NIV).

And we're to speak *persuasively* (aiming not simply to state the message but to prompt a response). 'Since, then, we know what it is to fear the Lord, we try to persuade men' (2 Cor. 5:11, NIV).

Love. Live. Speak. Those are our marching orders. Of course you've got your excuses ready. We all have. 'How can I love that fellow-believer? She's horrible!' 'Where can I escape to if I've got to live my life out before the watching eye of other people? I'm an introvert!' 'What role can I play in articulating the gospel? I'm hopeless with words!'

But nonetheless this is indeed our 'strategy'. It's not necessarily what we might have come up with, left to ourselves. But it's transparent ('we have renounced secret and shameful ways', 2 Cor. 4:2, NIV). It's honest ('we do not use deception'). It's authentic ('nor do we distort the word of God'). It's winning ('by setting forth the truth plainly we commend ourselves to everyone's conscience in the sight of God'). And most importantly, it's the strategy God has given us. And it's the means he is committed to using, as he assembles the cast for his glorious new creation.

GOD GIVES THE LIFE

People around us are always trying to make us feel empowered. Ever noticed that? Especially if they've got something to sell. 'Yes you can' is the watchword. '*Yes you can* lose ten pounds in a month' (if you buy into our weight loss programme). '*Yes you can* find the man of your dreams' (if you join our dating website). '*Yes you can* get that promotion you're after' (if you sign up for our assertiveness development course).

Well here's something you *can't* do. You can't give someone new life. You can't open spiritually blind eyes. You can't break the chains of slavery to sin. You can't grant repentance and faith. You can't transfer someone's citizenship from the kingdom of darkness to the kingdom of light.

Only the mighty Holy Spirit of God can do that. He's the major player in God's plan to 'bring all things in heaven and on earth under one head, even Christ'. So maybe it's time we started acting as though we believed it!

We need to get on our knees.

Ask God to provide opportunities for the gospel. 'Pray... that God may open a door for our message' (Col. 4:3, NIV).

Careful though. Are you ready for him to answer this prayer?!

Ask God to help you seek to commend the gospel. 'Pray... that whenever I speak, words may be given me...' (Eph. 6:19, NIV). It doesn't matter how clumsy with words you think you are – compared to other people. God can help you to speak the right ones at the right time.

And, of course, ask God to enable your hearer to respond to the gospel. Remember that hearing of Paul before Agrippa? 'Do you think in such a short time you can persuade me to be a Christian' asked Agrippa. 'Paul replied, "Short time or long – I pray God that not only you but all who are listening to me today may become what I am..."' (Acts 26:29, NIV).

You cannot do it. But yes, *he* can.

GOD RECEIVES THE GLORY

There's one more consequence of God being in the driving seat when it comes to the salvation of individuals. It's that whatever happens, the glory goes to him.

That's always been the plan. When tongues 'confess that Jesus Christ is Lord', says Paul, it is 'to the glory of God the Father' (Phil. 2:11, NIV). When he celebrates 'the grace that is reaching more and more people', it's because he dreams that it 'may cause thanksgiving to overflow to the glory of God' (2 Cor. 4:15, NIV). When Peter looks forward to what the 'proven genuineness of your faith' will accomplish, once refined, he relishes the thought that 'it may result in praise, glory and honour when Jesus Christ is revealed' (1 Pet. 1:7, NIV).

Every sinner who turns to Christ and receives forgiveness just increases the glory going to God.

Remember that, when someone you know professes faith, apparently as a result of your witness. There's no room for pride. God gave you the opportunity, he gave you the words, and he gave your friend the new birth.

But remember that too, when you see little apparent fruit from your efforts. When you're trying to be a faithful witness for Jesus, but see nothing happening in your friends month after month, year after year, discouragement can set in. Maybe a bit of guilt. Despair. Perhaps even embarrassment. It should not be. It's God – not you – who will grant repentance and faith.

SPEAK UP

I mustn't close this chapter without making one thing quite clear. The fact that God chooses who will receive life does not mean we can take our foot off the accelerator when it comes to speaking about Jesus. It *absolutely does not mean that!*

Imagine for a moment that I were to take you down to the left-luggage lockers at the airport down the road. There are rows of lockers there – maybe a hundred of them. All of them locked. And then I gave you a key and told you how things stand: that this is a master-key which is good for a number of these lockers, though not all. In fact probably just a handful of them would open with the key. But inside every one that opens, there's a stack of money. A fortune is waiting for you in each one.

What do you do? Try a couple, without success, and then get frustrated and just give up? You might, but probably not if you really believed me about the riches that are there waiting for you! If you *really* believed me, you'd try every door, muster every ounce of energy, keep going for as long as it took to release all the treasure locked up. Every failed attempt would be a spur to try another. In fact, you'd likely go back to the ones that didn't yield – again and again – just to see if the lock might loosen on a second, third, fourth attempt.

When Paul first arrived in Corinth, he found a mixed reception. Some 'opposed Paul and became abusive' (Acts 18:6, NIV). Others, though, 'believed and were baptised' (v. 8). It's not hard to imagine Paul weighing up whether to keep working this dry ground or move on to greener pastures. What sealed the deal for him, though, was an appearance of Jesus himself in a dream. The instruction was clear: 'Do not be afraid; keep on speaking, do not be silent' (v. 9). But it's the reason that's striking. Actually there were two reasons: (1) Jesus was going to stay by his side and keep him safe ('for I am with you and no one is going to attack and harm you'); and (2) Jesus had people marked out for salvation there ('because I have many people in this city', v. 10).

And so Paul stayed – for a further eighteen months. He kept speaking of Jesus. He kept going with that gospel key, trying the lockers of people's lives in his search for the treasure that is somebody whose name is written in the book of life. He kept going. Why? Because he believed that God was a big God, and had decided to grant repentance and faith to many of those around him.

Do you see how our human logic gets re-written? Our logic says: 'If God has already decided who his people are, what's the point of speaking?' God's logic says: 'Since God has already decided who his people are, keep speaking until you find them and have the joy of seeing them respond to the gospel of Jesus.'

࿇

God's plans for other people, then, are no disincentive to our sharing the gospel with them. Quite the reverse!

But what about his plans for us and our own decision-making? If God has a blueprint for our lives, how can we make sure we're reading it right and going through life according to that blueprint?

Unshrinking God in Decision-making

Mark was at a crossroads in his life. At twenty-one years old, he was – in the eyes of the law – very much an adult. But after years of wanting to get to that place, he was beginning to have second thoughts. Was he ready for the big wide world? He realised full-time education had come to feel a safe haven for him. The routines and relationships served to protect him from the need to make many really big life decisions. But he couldn't keep hiding in his island for ever. He'd have to get his feet wet in the big ocean of life at some point. He knew that. Trouble was, he'd been hoping to do it little by little, inching his way in. And yet, as things were going, it felt like he had no choice but to step off the end of the diving board and jump right in. And that was a scary prospect.

His first quandary was about the coming summer. Mark had been involved for some time with one of the dramatic societies and he'd always gone on the summer tour. The production for this summer was one he'd always wanted to do, and – given it was his last opportunity to work with the group – it would be a great opportunity to say farewell and cement some friendships he'd made there. There might even be some more chances to share his faith with his fellow Thespians. Going along was a no-brainer.

Until the dates were announced and it turned out it was going to conflict with camp. Mark had become a Christian at this camp and felt an intense loyalty to the team. He'd gone back year after year, first as a 'camper', then as 'assistant leader', and since last year as a 'leader'. It was a wonderful spiritual opportunity, and there'd been no question that he would be helping out again this summer.

But now he had to choose. Which was the right thing to do?

It was complicated by not knowing when he'd start his new job. And therein lay another can of worms. His family were in a bit of a mess at the moment and his instinct was to move back home for at least a year. He'd be able to help out practically, take care of the house, and – more than that – he knew that just his presence would be a real boost to Mum and Dad.

On the other hand, though, there was the question of how he'd support himself, indeed of his career. He'd be hard-pressed to find a job in his line anywhere close to home. And that effectively meant choosing either to put his career on hold and just pick up a local job, perhaps in retail, or to face a punishing commute which would most likely leave him drained of any ability to be helpful at home. Neither option was particularly attractive.

To move home or not to move home – that was the question.

And of course that decision was bound up with another: the cash question. Mark had received a small inheritance from his grandmother. It wasn't a huge amount, but it was enough to replace the lawnmower-on-four-wheels he optimistically called his 'car' with something a bit more reliable and comfortable. But was that really how he wanted to use this one-off cash-injection? He'd certainly need to get something if he moved home. Public transport around there was a joke. But in the city, well, it might even be possible to do without wheels at all. He could use it to start saving for a deposit on his first house. Or maybe give it to a missionary society he'd started to support. Or just put it in the bank for a rainy day.

Whichever way he went on the questions of where to live and what to do with the cash, though, the choice of which church to attend was also something he could no longer avoid thinking about. Was the church he'd been attending during his student days the right place to stick around at now? Was he being really spiritually fed? Were the church services places he could comfortably bring his friends too? Was there opportunity for someone like him to become more than just a 'passenger'? Was it just too big? But then, what about his friends? What would they think if he just jumped ship? And where would he go anyway? He knew there was no such thing as a perfect church!

But the one question that overshadowed all of these – the one in fact that dominated Mark's thinking – was the Emily question. They'd been together for eighteen months, and it was pretty clear that she saw them sharing their lives together. But he wasn't quite there. Was she 'the one' for him? How could he know? How long would it take to figure it out? And meanwhile, how big a part should she be playing in all the other decisions he had to make?'

So many questions! And so little clear guidance from God – or so it seemed. If God really had a plan for his life, how could he make sure he stayed within it?

What's your star sign? Do you know? Chances are that – however dubious you might say astrology is – you still know what sign of the zodiac you were born under. In fact, many heads have been scratched in recent years about the statistics of astrology belief. Around 25-30 per cent of the population in English-speaking western countries say they 'believe' in astrology. But here's the thing. Over 60 per cent of us actually read our horoscopes with some sort of regularity! How do we explain the gap between those two figures? Could it be, perhaps, that we give them more credence than we care to admit?

There are two spikes in the astrology belief statistics. One is women (three times more likely than men to consult their horoscopes). The other is young adults. Nearly half of 18-24-year olds check out the horoscope pages *at least* once a month. Those figures haven't changed much in a good few years. The reality is: even if many deny believing what they read, a staggering proportion of those taking their first steps in adult life routinely resort to reading up on what the stars have to say about their future.

Now why is that? I suspect it all comes down to decision-making. Not only are young adults in that age range generally just getting used to owning their own decisions for the first time; they're also faced with making some of the most *life-defining* decisions they'll ever make. From choice of belief-systems to choice of career, choice of partner to choice of where (and how) to live, the big decisions are coming thick and fast. And – understandably, given the mess they see others around them making of their lives – they don't necessarily trust themselves to get it right. So what a windfall it would be to find someone else who's effectively going to make the decisions for them. And if it's the very stars themselves who are doing it, that's even more of a bonus!

But it's not just young adults who are looking for someone else to shoulder responsibility for their decisions. We're all at it. From casual superstition ('look – it's a sign!') to routine consultations ('let me ask my life-coach about that'), we're all looking for ways to dodge the sheer stress of making choices. Maybe we're cautious by nature – we like to be absolutely sure for plumping for one option over another. Maybe we've simply been conditioned to living the life of consumer choice. The thought of closing down options for the future gives us palpitations. Maybe, in all honesty, we're really cowards. We're afraid of the consequences of getting it wrong. Maybe we're just plain lazy. We can't be bothered to think it all through and then act on our conclusions. But whichever it is, decision-making doesn't come easy to us.

The sad truth is: we Christians aren't that different. We might dress it up in different jargon, but by and large the same forces are in play deep in our hearts.

As a reality check, take a look (if you dare) at some dictionary definitions. These are all from the terminology of contemporary Christian decision-making.

Door *n.* 1. a hinged or sliding panel closing off an entrance. 2. an opportunity or direction in life, esp. referring to the apostle Paul's prayer request ('that God may open a door for our message…', Colossians 4:3, NIV). 3. *Pop. usage*: **God closed the door** an expression of laziness (= 'I had a go, but it didn't work out at the first attempt, and I couldn't be bothered to keep trying'). 4. **God opened the door** an expression of foolhardiness (= 'it worked out really easily so I figured it must be the right way to go').

Fleece *n.* 1. coat of wool covering a sheep or similar. 2. Ref. to Gideon's need for reassurance in asking God to soak a fleece with dew but not the surrounding ground and then vice versa (Judg. 6:36-40). 3. *Pop usage*: **putting out a fleece** an attempt to put God to the test (prohibited in Matthew 4:7) and bypass guidance of Bible and wisdom by asking for tangible signs to confirm a course of action under consideration (= 'rather than think through the wise approach and rejoice in the freedom God has given me I'm going to ask God to jump through some hoops for me in the mistaken belief that Gideon is held out as a positive model for decision-making').

Peace *n.* 1. absence of war. 2. sense of inner calm. 3. *Pop usage*: **feel a real peace about...** an expression of self-sufficiency (= 'rather than consult people around me to help my decision-making, as the Bible encourages, I choose instead to look within to a subjective state of mind and assure myself – for reasons as yet unclear – that this feeling of calm justifies the decision I am contemplating regardless of its defensibility on other grounds').

Verse *n.* 1. Short subdivision of a poem or Bible book. 2. *Pop usage*: **God gave me a verse** an expression of a naïve and irresponsible approach to Bible reading in which the calling to mind of a Bible verse with a tenuous verbal association to a current felt situation (not necessarily apparent to anybody other than the subject) is used to justify a course of action without reference to the meaning of the verse in the biblical context in which the Holy Spirit actually placed it (= 'I was so struck by the relevance of a particular word in a verse which popped into mind that I figured I didn't have to use my brain to understand the verse and decided to base a major life decision on a word association game my mind decided to play').

Wait *vb.* 1. To remain inactive for a period of time. 2. *Pop usage*: **wait on God** an expression of lack of trust in the sufficiency of the Bible for decision-making; and/or of cowardice related to consequences of a decision (= 'I couldn't bring myself to trust God in a decision which carried some apparent risks so I decided to do nothing for the time being and try to convince myself that that decision didn't really count as a decision').

Yes, yes, I know. I'm coming down pretty hard – probably *too* hard – on these sacred cows.

Of course God creates, or indeed closes off, opportunities in life. But we need to be a little wary of seeing opportunities that open up (or indeed knock-backs) as nudges from God to pursue (or give up pursuing) those possibilities. Remember Paul tried 'many times' to get to Rome, but was 'prevented from doing so' (Rom. 1:13, NIV). Why didn't he give up after the first time? Because he didn't see a first-time failure as a permanently closed door from God. On the other hand, the earthquake in Philippi gave Paul – literally – an open door to escape from prison: 'the prison doors flew open and everybody's chains came loose'. But he chose not to walk through that door, and that decision led to the conversion of the jailer and his whole family (Acts 16:25-34).

Of course God might choose to order events and circumstances in such an extraordinary way that we're left with no real option but to understand them as a signal from him. We'd be blind to miss it. But there is really no justification for *seeking* such a display. The early Christians in the Book of Acts were treated to the occasional rather dramatic divine steer. But it wasn't the norm, and in any case they were never encouraged to seek such a thing. Neither are we encouraged to imitate Gideon's request for a show of God's power. Remember: Gideon had *already* been told by God that God would make him victorious ('I will be with you, and you will strike down all the Midianites together', Judg. 6:16, NIV 1984). The fleece request was Gideon showing his unbelief. Not a great model!

Of course a believer may feel a sense of calm about some course of action he or she is contemplating. But a subjective emotional state is far from a sure guide. Think no further than Jesus in Gethsemane, 'sorrowful and troubled' (Matt. 26:37) as he contemplated submitting himself to the horror of Calvary. I bet you're glad he didn't take the lack of 'peace' about where he was heading as a reason to change course!

Of course God can work in our memories (or indeed the memories of our fellow-believers) to bring to mind a particular Bible verse. He has done so many times in my experience. And more significantly he did so when Jesus faced Satan in the wilderness (Luke 4:1-13). But we do need to examine these verses to see if they really *are* saying what we think they're saying, and are saying it *about* the thing we think they apply to. 'Test the spirits...' (1 John 4:1).

Of course there is a time for waiting to be sure, rather than ploughing ahead with a decision. Patience is part of the fruit of the Spirit. In fact there are a number of times in the Bible when this or that character could really have done with learning to wait on God a bit better. Look no further than Abraham and Sarah's failure to wait for God to give them the son they were looking forward to, instead coming up with their own plan (involving Abraham jumping into bed with Hagar to do the job, Gen. 16:1-4). But true Christian spirituality is an active spirituality. Remember what the Thessalonians were commended for: not just their faith, love and hope, but 'your *work* produced by faith, your *labour* prompted by love, and your *endurance* inspired by hope...' (1 Thess. 1:3, NIV).

In each case, do you see the danger? The danger is that we encourage or excuse what is really an attitude that dishonours God and falls short of what's appropriate for a Christian disciple!

So where can we go, then? Having demolished much of what underlies the popular approach to decision-making among contemporary Christians, let me suggest an approach that is in keeping with what we've learned about God in this book so far.

Remember how big God is? Our God really is in the driving seat. He hasn't relinquished the controls. He's personally and powerfully active in steering our lives towards the destination he has planned for us. He 'works out everything in conformity with the purpose of his will' (Eph. 1:11, NIV). His 'plan-will' is being executed second by second in minute detail, across the universe.

If you've really taken that on board, you're already more than half way to working through the key issues of Christian guidance. Because you've got what guidance really is. It's *not* about *us* trying to get a sneak preview of God's plan-will and acting accordingly. It's about *God* steering you and me and indeed all of creation in the direction he's decided to take it. Guidance is not primarily about information in my head to help me make decisions. It's about events in God's plan which he's gradually bringing to pass, and will continue to bring to pass however good or bad the decisions we make. He's taking things where he wants to take them.

When you remember that God really is in the driving seat, the pressure's off. All the anxiety we've been feeling about 'falling out of God's will' vanishes. All the paralysis which has taken hold of us while we wait for specific directions melts away. All the energy we've been investing in trying to listen out for God's voice can be channelled into other more productive uses (like fighting sin and loving others). It's just very, very freeing!

And yet. You may feel there are questions that need to be answered. After all, we still do need to make decisions. Even if guidance is not the most helpful word, surely we have a responsibility to seek to please God in the choices we make?

Yes we do. But a proper understanding of how God governs his world could transform the way we go about our decision-making.

MORE THOROUGH BIBLE READING

Once we've appreciated that God's plan-will is unlikely to be revealed to us ahead of time, and the only thing we've got access to is his ideal-will, what will that mean for us? Imagine an art-lover of eclectic taste who finds he has a free couple of hours. He decides to head out to the gallery. On arrival, he's disappointed to find the Renaissance exhibition closed. There's nothing he can see of it beyond a couple of admittedly fine specimens by the entrance. The Post-impressionists exhibition down the other end, however, is open. Now what's he going to do? He could spend the afternoon trying every door to the Renaissance exhibition, attempting to persuade a staff member to make an exception and let him in, looking for a cleaner who's willing to reveal the access code in exchange for a small backhander, complaining to the manager, procuring equipment that might allow him to abseil down from the roof and so peer in from the windows, or some such activity. Or he could look at the limited time available, accept that there's no way in to the Renaissance exhibition, and therefore decide to go and feast his eyes on the Cezannes, the Gauguins and the van Goghs in the exhibition that's open. Which sounds like the better plan?

The Bible is an exhibition of God's ideal-will. And it's open to all comers. But as long as we think there's some prospect of getting access to his plan-will, we'll always be distracted. We'll find ourselves more excited about exploring those possible ways to what's closed to us than simply enjoying what is available. Once we've given up our quest for that back door, and so recognise the Bible as the God-given resource where Christian decision-making starts and finishes, we'll find it speaks into our lives with power and clarity we never appreciated before.

Wait a minute. The place where decision-making starts? Surely not! Surely prayer is where it starts, isn't it? Well, no. Good decision-making for believers starts with getting a grasp of the Bible. Bible comes before even prayer. Why? Because we tend to pray about our decisions only when we see a decision needs to be made. Whereas getting to know the Bible needs to start way before that. A lot of decision-making is about training our *instincts* to think in line with God's thoughts. And that takes time in his Word – years and years of it. So if you care about the decisions you need to make in years to come, get into your Bible *now*!

And the place where it ends? Surely there are other helpful things we need to do as well as read the Bible? Yes there are, and we'll come to that. But in a real sense, we don't need to go beyond the Bible: 'All Scripture is God-breathed and is useful for teaching, rebuking, correcting and training in righteousness, *so that the man of God may be thoroughly equipped for every good work*' (2 Tim. 3:16, NIV).

So what does that look like in practice? Take a decision most people will have to make: whether to get married, and if so, to whom? The Bible gives us plenty of help with working out God's ideal-will.

Whether we marry or not is a matter of preference and opportunity. Do you want to get married? Does someone want to marry you? Then go to it!

Sometimes Christians might wonder, 'Do I have the gift of singleness?' They're using the language of Paul ('each of you has your own *gift* from God; one has this *gift*, another has that', 1 Cor. 7:7, NIV), but not in quite the way that Paul uses it. What they're really asking is about one of three things: capacity ('Am I actually capable of living in celibacy?'); contentment ('Could I truly have a full and happy life without the companionship of a spouse?'); or the crystal ball ('Does my future involve life-long singleness or is there somebody who will come into my life at some point'). And wondering on the basis of these questions whether – or with how much vigour – they should look for a marriage partner.

In fact, it's very easy to know if you have the gift of singleness. If you are currently single, you have it. If you are not, you don't. Yes, it really is that simple. When Paul talks about singleness and marriage as gifts, he's not referring to a state that God has awarded us for life, but without actually having the decency to tell us. He's simply referring to both marriage (and specifically the expression of sexuality within marriage) and singleness (specifically the freedom from unconquerable sexual temptation as a single person) as gifts conferred by God. They go with the turf, not with the individual. And indeed they may change (as a rabbi, Paul was probably once married – hence perhaps his ability to talk with such authority about both gifts).

The bottom-line is: both singleness and marriage are gifts from God. They both bring benefits (the married person does not normally need to 'burn with passion', v. 9; the unmarried can be spared 'many troubles', v. 28, as well as find greater gospel opportunities). And they both have much to commend them. So they're matters of preference and opportunity.

That much goes for those who have never been married or have been widowed. For those who are already married, it's a 'no' to marrying: Christians are not to engage in polygamy. For those who are divorced, it's a bit trickier, as there are a number of texts that need to be put together, and I'm not going to try to summarise them in a paragraph!

So much for *whether* to marry. What about *whom* to marry? Does the Bible have anything to say to that? Well, actually yes! For one thing, we're to marry somebody of the opposite sex (same-sex marriages might be recognised by the state, but they're foreign to the Bible's blueprint for marriage – Gen. 2:24). Then again, we're to marry someone we're not closely related to (incest is out – Lev. 18). More than that, the person we're marrying must not be already married themselves, or indeed in need of reconciliation to someone they have been married to in the past (Mark 10:11-12). Last, but not least, our spouse needs to be someone who shares our Christian convictions (1 Cor. 7:39; 2 Cor. 6:14).

Beyond these principles, though, there is freedom. Of course, we'll still want to exercise discernment in a decision of whether and/or whom to marry. It's possible to be very foolish. But poor judgement is not the same as disobedience!

MORE MATURE PRAYER

As my holiday destination determines what clothes I'll pack in preparation, so what I conceive of as the destination of my life will shape the prayers I pray as I face the rest of my life.

Where is God steering my life? We've seen that, although God has a plan for our lives, he doesn't reveal the details of that plan in advance. But that's not to say that he doesn't reveal *any* of it! (Remember those couple of masterpieces on view even at the closed exhibition!) In fact, we do know a few major landmarks. The biggest of all is this: that God's great, cosmic, long-term, stated plan for everything and everybody is 'to bring all things in heaven and on earth together under one head – even Christ' (Eph. 1:10, NIV).

That's the overall scheme. But actually we know more than that. We know too that believers have a specific part in that process: 'It is God's will that you should *be sanctified*' (ie 'made holy', 1 Thess. 4:3, NIV). 'He chose us... *to be holy and blameless* in his sight' (Eph. 1:4, NIV). We need the 'knowledge of God's will... so that you may *live a life worthy of the Lord* and may please him in every way' (Col. 1:9-10, NIV).

Are you getting the picture? This is God's plan for our lives. It's the destination towards which he's steering us.

If we think the place God is taking us is total happiness in the here and now, our prayers concerning the decisions before us will most likely be filled with requests for the things we think will make us happy. 'Lord, please help me to figure out who I should ask out – Katie or Lisa – so that I can end up with the perfect girl for me.' If we think God is mainly concerned with making sure we have good options and a real sense of fulfilment, we'll probably pray for things tending in that direction. 'Lord please give me a job – don't mind what, as long as it's stimulating and makes me feel like I'm in the right place.' If we think God is chiefly interested in making us prosper materially, we'll pray accordingly. 'Lord, point me towards a good financial adviser who will set me up for the most comfortable possible retirement.'

But it's not. God's plan for us is to take us towards holiness, towards the place where our lives really are pleasing to him. Those prayers are not necessarily wrong ones to pray, but if those are the main kind of prayers we pray, then our prayer life is a pretty immature one. Our prayers need to change.

You want to know whether to ask out Katie or Lisa? How about praying: 'Lord, please help me to discern which of these girls will help me to become more like Christ; to recognise who I could partner with in a marriage that would give glory to you; to figure out which of them will provide a godly model to any children you might send.' That's a mature prayer, a prayer shaped by God's primary purposes for you.

You're thinking about a change of job or career? What about this: 'Lord, please provide a job that provides for the needs of my family, with a boss that I can respect, an environment where I can demonstrate and speak about the love of Christ with my colleagues and a schedule which makes it easy for me to spend time with you in Bible-study and prayer and to serve my family and my fellow believers in my local church.' That's a mature prayer, a prayer with the right focus.

You're unsure how to plan for your retirement? Try: 'Lord, help me to discern the right balance between responsible saving and generosity to others. Take away my anxiety about money and teach me to trust in your provision. Help me to be a good steward and to make prudent choices about where and how to invest, so that I don't need to be a burden on others.' Again it's a mature prayer that's driven by God's goal for us.

It's one thing, you see, to add 'your will be done', as perhaps we sometimes do, as a kind of formula to close out our prayers. It's quite another to pray prayers *which are themselves in keeping with what we know of God's will*. They're prayers which in and of themselves are saying 'your will be done!'

And that's where we'll get to if we pay attention to where God is taking us.

MORE PLENTIFUL SUPPLY OF WISDOM

How do you get to work (or your place of study or whatever) each day? Walk? Bus? Train? Cycle? Drive? For many of us, there's a choice of route – which roads to use, which bus stop to get off, which train to catch. Maybe the first time you made the journey, you didn't know the best route. But little by little you came to notice that if you leave home after 7.45, York Street is a nightmare for traffic; much better to use Plymouth Avenue. Or that the 8.03 train always has some spare seats, which is more than can be said for the 7.53. Or if you get off the bus one stop earlier you save seven minutes on your journey time *and* you don't have to risk your life crossing the road at that terrifying junction. Little by little, you've taken on board the observations and adjusted your journey accordingly.

It's called wisdom. And there are only two ways of getting it: the slow way and the quick way. The slow way is just to keep on observing life yourself. Seeing what tends to result from this or that situation. Taking note of the disastrous consequences – or indeed the wonderful consequences – which follow from the decisions people make, or the things they say, or the people they spend time with or the habits they form, and so on. And then prayerfully and reflectively applying the principles to your own decision, speaking, friendships, habits, etc.

It's slow because most of us are busy and not all of us are particularly observant. So it takes years, indeed decades, to become wise this way.

Then there's the quick way. And that's to find other people who have been observing and learning for longer than us – and tap into their wisdom! In some areas of life an approach like that is called cheating, plagiarism, or plain cheek. But when it comes to wisdom, different rules apply. The Bible says wisdom is so valuable we'd be well advised to procure it any way we can!

> Wisdom is supreme; therefore get wisdom. Though it cost all you have, get understanding.

> Esteem her, and she will exalt you; embrace her, and she will honour you.

> She will set a garland of grace on your head and present you with a crown of splendour. (Prov. 4:7-9, NIV 1984)

No wonder, then, that the same book of Proverbs provides so many encouragements to seek out the advice of others (e.g. 'The way of a fool is right in his own eyes, but a wise man listens to advice', Prov. 12:15). In fact, it gets better. The book itself is full of examples of such collected wisdom and advice: how to live in a way that's in step with the patterns of cause and effect which are the norm in God's world. So there's another route to getting wise.

Of all the choices Christians find themselves scratching their heads about, the majority are going to be situations where – whichever option they choose – they'll be consistent with biblical instructions. They're therefore areas of freedom, so they're areas where wisdom is required. But the great news is: that wisdom is available! Most Christians will have a Christian friend, a colleague, a mentor, a prayer partner, a parent, a small group leader, a pastor, or just someone they know from church who looks like they've been round the block a few times and seems to speak good sense. So whatever the issue – a tricky situation at work, a finely balanced call they need to make as parents, a ministry they've been asked to help with at church, a sensible approach to fighting some specific sin – pick up the phone!

Let's go back to the example of the choice of a marriage partner. We've seen the biblical principles. What further advice might a wise Christian add to the mix?

- Maybe they'll raise questions about the person's spiritual background. They'll advise you to be cautious in marrying someone who's on a different page theologically, or who's a much less mature believer.

- Perhaps they'll suggest you watch how your partner treats other people. When the first flush of romance fades, he or she will likely treat you the same way!

- Possibly they'll ask questions about leadership and submission. Is she someone you could easily lead? Is he someone you could easily submit to?

- They'll likely encourage you to find out what your friends and your parents really think about the two of you getting together – and to pay attention to it!

The point is, we are richly blessed. In our churches God has given us a precious gift. We have brothers and sisters who are both aware of God's purposes for his people and have seen – maybe more than we have – where decisions taken today lead tomorrow. We'd be fools not to enjoy the benefit.

MORE INITIATIVE

'Buridan's Ass' is a philosophical conundrum named after a medieval French philosopher. It imagines a hungry donkey standing exactly midway between two equally tasty-looking piles of fresh hay. Which will it choose? Because it needs a reason to choose one over another – and such a reason is lacking – will not the donkey simply starve to death through indecision? Even today, 700 years after Buridan, philosophy students investigating determinism and free will are routinely set this as a problem to work through.

Many Christians today behave, if you don't mind my saying, like Buridan's Asses. Waiting as they are for God to reveal the details of his plan, they simply do nothing. (Or – to be more accurate – they decide to keep doing what they are currently doing.) They're too afraid of making a mistake they'll have to live with, or too overwhelmed by the number of choices on offer, or too defined by the baggage of their past, or too worried about missing out on God's plan. So indecision is the order of the day.

The great thing about God's plan is that it's impossible to exit from it! Remember: God 'works out everything in conformity with the purpose of his will' (Eph. 1:11, NIV). So we can relax about the choices we make. Once we've established the course of action is consistent with God's ideal-will as revealed in the Bible, and we've prayed for discernment, and we've sought out wisdom on the issue, it's time to show some initiative. It's time to decide! To delay a decision *may* be a prudent thing, allowing more time to think it through. But it's just as likely – or indeed more so – to be an expression of unbelief. It's tantamount to saying, 'Lord, I know you *say* that in all things you work for the good of those who love you, but I don't really trust you to do that in *this* case.'

So where does that leave you in the decisions that you're facing? Is it time to dig into the Bible and search out God's ideals that need to underpin your decision? Or time to get on your knees and pray for God to shape your thinking and your approach? Perhaps it's time to be thinking who you can involve in the decision to give you a headstart in your wisdom. Or perhaps the very fact that you've read this far suggests the time has come to stop procrastinating and take that decision – however risky it might seem!

Whatever your next step is, remember this: the future rests on more than your decisions. There's another player in this game. 'In their hearts, humans plan their course, the Lord establishes their steps' (Prov. 16:9, NIV).

6

Unshrinking God in Prayer

As with most blow-ups, the spark was a relatively trivial matter. Caroline had asked the others in her prayer triplet to pray about a job interview. It was a prestigious company she was looking to work for, but she'd done work experience with them in the summer and it was their suggestion that she apply for a permanent position after graduation. Caroline had rarely experienced any kind of failure in her life, and when she was told – within just forty-eight hours – that she hadn't made the shortlist, she took it hard. Indignation: that was the only word to describe her reaction. The company got it – they shouldn't have raised her hopes and wasted her time. Her friends got it – they shouldn't have encouraged her to go for it. And sadly the others in her prayer triplet got it too – the group's prayers had given her complete confidence that her future with the company was secure: it came with a heaven-backed guarantee.

'What's the point of praying, if God doesn't answer?' she'd fumed. 'We've been meeting week after week for over a year, and what have we got to show for our prayers? We prayed for your brother, Jane, when he went off to Africa, and he came home without a hand. We prayed for unity in your church, Sarah, and there was a leadership split. And now we pray for something pretty simple like a job interview and I get turned down. Clearly God's decided what he's going to do, and that's the end of the matter. Maybe he does what we ask sometimes if he agrees with our prayers, but how is that actually answering the prayers, if he was planning to do it all along? I know we have a lot of fun together, but it feels like the only reason we pray is because that's what Christians are supposed to do. I'm sorry – that's just not good enough for me.'

'Hang on a minute, Caroline, that's not right', Sarah said. Of course God doesn't have a fixed plan. It can't all be set in stone already. Why would he want us to ask him for things unless he was prepared to change his mind? Come on Caroline, you know prayer changes things. I don't know, maybe we just didn't pray with enough faith about your job interview and those other things.

'Oh I see', said Caroline, raising her voice now. 'So it's all my fault. It's all down to my faith being too weak. Thanks for laying it all on me.'

It was time for Jane to weigh in.

'Caroline, that's not what she said. It's just that there could be any number of reasons why God didn't answer that particular prayer. Prayer isn't just about God doing things for us, you know. It's about God changing who we are and learning to trust him and relate to him.'

'Exactly', said Caroline. 'The whole thing is just a charade. Our prayers don't get answered in a concrete way. We've just been kidding ourselves.'

She paused.

'I'm sorry. I don't want to hurt you, but I just can't do this any more.'

And with that, she picked up her coat and walked out.

It was big knock for Jane. It wasn't until they stopped meeting that she realised just how reliant she was on her prayer triplet for spiritual support. She desperately wanted to sort out Caroline's issues once and for all. But the more she thought about it, the more she tied herself up in knots.

Did God really answer prayer? Or had she been fooling herself all the way along. After all, suppose one of the other candidates for the job had also prayed for success, as well as Caroline. God couldn't simultaneously answer both prayers, could he? Somebody was going to be disappointed. It was the same when you prayed for the weather: it's all very well praying for a nice sunny day for a wedding, but what about the farmer down the road who's praying for rain for his crops? God would have to choose, wouldn't he? It could only be one or the other. It couldn't be both.

But then again, what if it was neither? Sarah had talked about things being not 'set in stone', but was that right? Surely God had in fact mapped everything out. Wasn't that the whole point about God and his plans? Didn't the Bible talk about God being the one who 'works all things according to the purpose of his will'? In which case the result of Caroline's job interview was predetermined a long time ago. In fact, how could God allow himself to be influenced by mere human beings? If God has all the wisdom and all the knowledge, he knows what the right thing to do is far better than us. He's not going to change his mind. So he doesn't need suggestions or nudges from us. But, if that's the case, then where does prayer fit in? What place is there for 'ask and you shall be given'? How can our prayers actually change anything?

Come to think of it, if God had indeed decided everything, then wouldn't that have to include whether the prayer triplet was going to pray, and what they prayed about? In which case, what was the point of even bothering to think about it? They'd just be pawns in the great steamroller of God's unfolding will.

Or was it in fact more about the person praying than the thing prayed for? Jane felt Caroline had misunderstood her words about God using the experience of prayer to mature people. She hadn't meant to imply that was all there was to prayer. But maybe that was indeed the main point. Was prayer basically God's way of getting people to think about and articulate what they really wanted and so get more serious about their faith and their future? Was it simply that it brought things to the front of our minds so that we aimed at them more deliberately and effectively answered our own prayers?

Democracy's a funny thing. All over the world there are people living under oppressive regimes who long for a say in where their country is heading. On the day they're allowed to vote for their government of choice – if such a day ever comes – nothing on earth will keep them from that ballot box! And yet in nations where democratic ideals have long been part of the wallpaper of life, most citizens rarely show up on election day, unless compelled to (take a bow, Australia!) Maybe they'll drop by the polling station on the way home from work; probably when it comes to it, they'll just be too tired so will skip it in favour of an extra half-hour in front of the TV.

For one, the chance to speak their mind is itself all the incentive to they need to vote. For another, the opposite is true: all they can think about is the other people who have a similar opportunity and who collectively minimise the significance of their own preference. 'What's the point?' they ask themselves. 'What difference will a single vote make to anything?'

It's odd that giving people their own personal soapbox from which to speak like this should lead to such different reactions.

But it's even more anomalous that God's provision of a direct line to the creator of the universe can also – on occasion – lead to Christian believers going in similarly different directions.

Because we do, don't we? Many of us know people for whom prayer seems to be as natural as breathing. They've never lost the sense of privilege in being able to sidle up to their heavenly father and open up their hearts to him. They pray, and keep praying, because – well because they *can*! If you're anything like most of us, though, you yourself couldn't be more different. For most of us, the sky needs to be falling down around us before we'll squeeze out five minutes from our day's busy schedule to talk to God. Yes, there's the occasional outbreak of serious prayer activity, induced maybe by a dose of guilt or possibly a powerful sermon. But the ramp-up doesn't last. It's soon back to business as usual.

Why is it like this? There are any number of ways of explaining our prayerlessness relative to those super-spiritual people we know.

TEMPERAMENT

One big one is the issue of temperament and personality. The typical extrovert, for example, often has great difficulty with prayer. The bias he or she will often have towards activity and doing can make cultivating an inner life hard for them. They find it extraordinarily challenging to get one-on-one with God for more than a brief time. And even when they do, they'll rarely experience those peaks of inspiration and spiritual highs they hear their more introverted friends talk about, which just deepens their level of guilt and disillusionment.

Even if not extroverted, many find a real difficulty in engaging on a deep level about any of their feelings. Many grew up with cold or distant parents, or at least in an environment where they weren't encouraged to express feelings. Well, little wonder they find it hard to engage with God on a deep level.

Each of us has our own battles here. The perfectionist will tend to insist on the perfect circumstances being in place before they engage with God: the right mood, the right place, the right time – everything has to be 'just so' before they can approach their heavenly father. Which, of course, it rarely is.

Those with a depressive personality will often find that pretty much anything – including and maybe especially prayer – requires more emotional energy than they can possibly muster. It's just too high a mountain to conquer.

One reason why resolutions of fresh starts in the prayer department so often fail is that the resolver has simply failed to address issues of his or her temperament. So they've failed to think through appropriate mechanisms which will prompt and spur them to pray. For example...

- Are you an extrovert? Try seeking out others to pray with regularly!

- Short attention span and wandering mind? How about saying your prayers out loud!

- Difficulties in engaging on a deep level? Try pen-and-paper prayers!

- Depressive tendencies? Make use of the Bible's prayers and psalms, or maybe some music on your MP3 player.

DISILLUSIONMENT

Disillusionment is another reason many find themselves limping along in their prayer lives. It may be a disillusionment with the experience itself. Their expectations of sweet intimacy and quasi-mystical communion with God fail to convert to reality. In fact, they feel barely any sense of God's presence at all. It feels like their prayers are just bouncing off the ceiling!

It's all a serious let-down considering what they've been led to expect by the books they've read, the preachers they've listened to and the friends they've observed.

And that's not all. On top of the disappointment from unmet expectations of feeling the warm presence of God, further disillusionment sets in when the requests they've made of God don't lead to the results they were after. 'Ask and it will be given to you' is the promise they remember from Jesus. Well, they've asked. Perhaps repeatedly. Perhaps for a long time. But it's not happening.

'So what's the point?' they ask themselves. Lack of results leads to disillusionment. And disillusionment hardens into prayer defeatism.

UNBELIEF

But let's not miss what's really going on under the surface in these attitudes. They seem quite reasonable, especially to a typical product of our generation.

The world we know is constantly inviting us to evade responsibility. The criminal is really a victim of society: it's the rest of us who are to blame for his actions. We let him down. The alcoholic learnt her ways in her family – how could she escape their way of coping with life's burdens. It's not her fault. The sexual deviant is a prisoner of his own biology. He was genetically programmed to look for pleasure where he does. He can't help it.

We may differ in how much credence we give to these attitudes. But we can't miss the general drift of our culture towards evading responsibility for our own actions. What we might miss is just how much we ourselves are influenced by it. We're always on the lookout for something outside ourselves to blame.

Coming back to our prayer lives, for example, our temperament, may help us to give some *context* to our struggle with regular and sustained prayer. But it can't excuse it. Our past experience with prayer may *describe* the path we've trodden away from prayer. But it doesn't justify it.

The ultimate explanation for the prayerlessness of any one of us is always the same. We simply fail to believe. Our hearts are cold towards God. We claim to have a relationship with him, but we fail to live it out. We speak of trusting him and depending upon him, but our inclinations are really towards self-reliance. In practice we're all – to some degree – spiritual survivalists: we've set up a life in which – come what may – we can meet all our needs from our own resources. Or so we think.

CONFUSION
But there's another factor which might be in play here. And this is where we come to the meat of this chapter. OK,

it may well be an excuse rather than a reason – see above! – but it's still a reality that many of us struggle with the *logic* of just how prayer works.

If God has already decided what to do, why bother praying? In Isaiah 46:9-10, we read: 'I am God and there is none like me, declaring the end from the beginning and from ancient times things not yet done, saying, "My counsel shall stand, and I will accomplish all my purpose"'. But if things really are that fixed, then what possible impact can my prayers have? Prayer is surely a meaningless waste of time, isn't it?

So maybe God does in fact change his mind when we pray. In Amos 7:3, we come across one of a number occasions in the Bible where God is described as relenting. God has promised judgement on his people. Amos pleads with God not to. And then in response to this comes the line: 'The LORD relented.' Maybe then God really is a bit more open to suggestion and influence than we thought. In which case, there's plenty of motivation to pray, but there are some even trickier questions to deal with.

What happens if two people pray simultaneously for diametrically opposite things? Like the girl who prays she'll get that great job in the city, while her mother meanwhile is praying she'll get something local so she'll stay close by. What will the God who is 'open to suggestion and influence' do then? Or if I pray for a certain outcome from an event I think is yet to happen, but which in fact is already done and dusted. Like when I pray as requested for my friend's operation just as he's going under at 2pm, only to find that they switched the order and the did the procedure at 11am. What happens then? Or when I ask for two things I believe are separate but actually are linked and in fact logically impossible (I pray for gorgeous weather for Jim and Angela's wedding, and I pray for rain for Farmer Cyril, not realising that Jim and Angela's wedding is actually taking place at the farm). Trickiest of all, what happens when, having prayed, I don't get the answer I was looking for. What should I conclude? That my faith is lacking? That I've reached my quota for answered prayers?

Is there a middle road, then? Maybe it's worth praying because God does listen and take account of *some* prayers. But if that's right, if God does act in response to certain prayers – the prayers which are in accordance with his will, perhaps – then how does that really help? I mean, he was always going to do that anyway, wasn't he? If we pray for somebody to become a Christian, then if they're on God's list for salvation, they're bound to get converted anyway; and if not then it's a dead cert nothing's going to happen. So we're back where we started: what's the point? Why not just pray, 'Your will be done, God!' – and be done with it?

It's easy to get tied up in knots when it comes to questions like these. And of course, the wonder of speaking to our heavenly Father can get forgotten in all the confusion over how exactly our prayers and God's will fit together.

We saw in a previous chapter how God's being in charge of people getting saved didn't kill Paul's passion to get the gospel out. Quite the reverse: in Acts 18:9-10 God's past decision to include certain people in his plans was the *motivation* for Paul speaking. '...Go on speaking, Paul... for I have many in this city who are my people' – which prompts him to stay another eighteen months in Corinth.

So is there any analogy when it comes to prayer? In what ways might God's being in the driving seat actually *encourage* – rather than discourage – us from praying?

Let me suggest a couple of ways.

EXPERIENCING GOD'S PLAN FOR US

The first is that the practice of praying is itself the fullest experience available to us of God's eternal plans for us!

Think about why it is you might pray on any particular occasion. Is it because of your *circumstances*? You're in a situation where things seem out of control, so you ask God to sort things. Is it because of a *command*? You remember those instructions from Paul, 'Be... faithful in prayer' (Rom. 12:12, NIV). Or: 'Do not be anxious about anything, but in every situation, by prayer and petition, with thanksgiving, present your requests to God' (Phil. 4:6, NIV). Is it because of *how you feel*? You see something awful – or perhaps something wonderful – that makes you want to talk to God. Is it because of *routine*? 'It's 7.20am. Time for my devotions.' Or: 'The food's served. We always pray before we eat.'

Maybe it's time to think bigger.

Here's a thought. If you were asked to summarise your spiritual biography, what might you include? Something about your upbringing and early impressions of the Christian faith? Maybe something about a drift away? Maybe a mention of the influence of a friend or a speaker or a book which made you re-evaluate? A comment about how and where you came to Christ and what life has been like since?

It might all be true. But have you ever thought how 'me-focused' it is? What would happen if you shifted the perspective and told it all from a God's-eye view? How about this:

'God saw me before I was born, in fact before the universe even existed. (He can do that, being God.) And he decided – for reasons known only to himself – that he wanted to get to know me. So he marked me out as one of the people he would bring into his family – I was to be a younger brother to his own son!

There was much to be done, though. First the universe had to be created. Then a habitat for human beings ('earth') needed to brought into being. And my species had to be introduced into this habitat. Human history had to begin and to be maintained.

That was the easy bit. The harder thing was dealing with the situation when – along with the entire human race – I rejected the idea of being friends with God. That required much work, not least the humiliation of God's son entering the human world and submitting even to death, before coming out victorious on the other side of it.

But there was more. God sent his Spirit to tell me about himself ('the Bible') and to give me a new heart that wanted to get to know him. As the people he'd arranged to introduce me to Jesus did their work, this Spirit enabled me to accept what they said as true and to start trusting God for my spiritual future. As I did so, he wiped away the guilty record I had for rejecting him as I had done, included me as a member of his family and made me want to serve him and get to know him better.

Every single barrier to relationship has been – or is being – cleared away for a beautiful relationship between me and God. And one day nothing at all will stand in the way of it.'

Well, it's a slightly different way of telling the story, to be sure! But it's the way God tells it. The above is not much more than a loose paraphrase of the first half of Ephesians 1.

But what comes out of it more clearly than anything is that *each of us has been made by God, for relationship with God.* In God's plans, which he went to some considerable pains to bring to pass, the very reason we exist is that we may relate to God.

That's why Jesus can simply assume that his followers will pray ('When you pray...', Matt. 6:5). A non-praying Christian believer is a contradiction in terms – like a schoolteacher who refuses to have anything to do with children, or a butcher who won't touch meat, or a librarian who stays away from books! Ducks quack. Cows moo. Horses neigh. Christians PRAY!

A sprinter might reach the pinnacle of his or her career in running at the Olympics. 'This is what all the gruelling training and preparation was about', she thinks as she steps out onto the track before the gaze of the world. An astronaut might achieve his purpose as he blasts off and leaves earth's atmosphere behind. 'This is the culmination of all the years of study, the fitness regime, the endless drills and exercises', he says to himself at that moment. A soldier thinks similarly as she leaves the base en route to the battle field for the first time. 'This is the moment of truth – the reason the army has invested in me and trained me and equipped me', she thinks as she ponders the conflict ahead.

So it is for the Christian believer in prayer. It is what we were made for: relating to our heavenly father. It is the closest experience we will have this side of glory to the fulfilment of God's plans for us which stretch back to before time began. And unlike the sprinter, the astronaut and the soldier, it's available 24/7. Right this minute, you could turn to God in prayer and experience what in God's purposes you were made for!

FURTHERING GOD'S PLANS

But there's a second big motivation to pray which comes from God's purposes. It's this. When we pray, we're actually furthering God's plans for the world.

We've seen already that God's choosing of his people, far from being a disincentive to evangelism, is actually a spur to it. But the truth is: that shouldn't surprise us. Because it is through human means that God normally works in the world. When God wants to bring some blessing to someone, he doesn't just press buttons on some divine remote control. No, he involves people like you and me in bringing his blessings to the world.

There's an old story told about a man whose town was flooding. Evacuation was ordered. And his neighbours offered him a place in their car. 'Don't worry', said the man. 'God will look after me'.

The floods rose, and someone in a canoe paddled by. He too asked the man to jump in with him. 'Don't worry', said the man. 'God will look after me'.

The water kept rising, until eventually the man was forced to the roof of his house.

When God works, his standard operating procedure is to involve us. And one of the chief ways he involves us is through our prayers.

The apostle Paul helps us to think this through. In 2 Corinthians 1, he spends some time describing some of the trials he has run into during his ministry. Death, he says, has been a real risk. But thus far, he has evaded the worst. Why? Is it that he's just got lucky? No, it's because God 'has delivered us from such a deadly peril' (2 Cor. 1:10, NIV).

But now he starts to look ahead to the future. It turns out he's feeling fairly confident: '...and he [God] will deliver us again.' Paul is sure that God will keep looking after him. The question is: how? Have a look at what he writes.

> On him we have set our hope that he will continue to deliver us, *as you help us by your prayers.* Then many will give thanks on our behalf for the gracious favour granted us in answer to the prayers of many. (2 Cor. 1:10b-11, NIV)

That might be surprising. We tend to pit action against prayer. But not Paul. The Corinthians can actually help Paul *by* praying (not as well as, or instead of, praying). The way God will bring his deliverance to Paul and his ministry colleagues is by people praying for him. Why? Because people praying for him is the route to God bringing his blessings. Hence the confirmation in the following sentence: God's gracious favour 'will be granted in answer to the prayers of many'.

What do we learn here about the logic of prayer? The key lesson is that God turns his plans into reality by listening to – and responding to – our prayers.

In the bigger picture of course, even the prayers we pray are part of his plan. He's a big God. So big that he can take our requests to him, and his responses to them, and weave them into the plan he has always had for the world.

Again and again in the Bible, we read of God doing exactly that. When Israel worships a golden calf, for example, God is incensed. 'Now leave me alone', he tells Moses, 'so that my anger may burn against them and that I may destroy them' (Exod. 32:10, NIV). But Moses prays. He reminds God of his actions for Israel so far, the consequences for God's reputation if he destroys them, and indeed his promises about Israel in past generations. And he pleads with God for them: 'Turn from your fierce anger; relent and do not bring disaster on your people' (v. 12). In response to which, we read: 'Then the LORD relented and did not bring on his people the disaster he had threatened' (v. 14).

Be clear on this. God was already committed to seeing through his plans for Israel. He hadn't forgotten his promises to Abraham about them! But he chose to continue to bless them – rather than destroy them as he threatened – *in response to* the prayers of Moses.

So which is it? Did God stay with Israel because Moses prayed – or because he'd already decided to? Answer: yes, and yes! It's not a neat answer that satisfies our human logic. The fact that God is so big that he can run history like this blows our minds! But then, shouldn't we expect our minds to be blown from time to time by the God who holds the world in the palm of his hands?

It's all very humbling. But the immediate point is this: the way God has set up the world, he's committed himself to acting as he hears his people praying. And the sooner we get this, the better. Because we'll realise God's overarching plan-will is not a disincentive to prayer, but an enormous motivation. We don't pray just because we *can* – although that should be enough reason for us. We pray because *our prayers lead to God working.*

What a privilege to be involved in God furthering his plans for the world like this!

So will you pray? As Christian believers, we never lose sight of the extraordinary privilege of prayer. The God who holds the furthest reaches of the universe in his hands is interested in the most minute and intimate details of your life and mine. He invites us to call him Father and to bring our needs to him.

So again, will you pray? And I mean *really* pray? I imagine you'll answer in the affirmative, but it may be that you could do with a reminder of what Christian prayer really looks like. I'm talking specifically about asking prayers (as opposed to thanking prayers, adoring prayers and sin-confessing prayers). But there are a few pretty important things to note if we're going to pray the way God wants to hear us.

HOW TO TALK TO GOD THE WAY HE LIKES TO LISTEN

1. PRAY WITH HONESTY

It's easy to get worried about saying exactly the right words, dotting every theological 'i' and crossing every 't'. Or to start questioning your motivations as you speak to God. Or to hold back because we don't know if this or that is something we really should be praying for. Relax! God knows it all. And his Spirit will work to 'translate' your prayers before God answers them. *Remember: God is your heavenly father who simply loves to hear his children speak to him.* 'We do not know what we ought to pray for, but the Spirit himself intercedes for us through wordless groans' (Rom. 8:26, NIV).

2. PRAY WITH CONFIDENCE

Tentative prayer breathes a lack of trust in God's ability to answer or his interest in the concerns of his children. God may or may not answer in exactly the way we want him to answer. But he will answer! And when he does, your prayers will have been part of the jigsaw of history itself. *Remember: God is the powerful creator and sustainer of the universe who can do anything.* Hence the encouragement of James: 'When you ask, you must believe and not doubt…' (James 1:6, NIV).

3. PRAY WITH PERSEVERANCE

You've asked once and seen no answer. So… what? You're going to give up, just like that? You didn't give up that easily when you asked for that pet, or that gizmo, or that bike, did you? So why would you throw in the towel so easily with God? He is teaching us patience and seeing how much our hearts are in it. *Remember: God is looking to make us more like Jesus – and growing in patience is part of that.* Take note of the example of that persistent widow in Jesus' parable and the comment about God that follows: 'will not God give justice to his elect, who cry to him day and night?' (Luke 18:7).

4. PRAY WITH HUMILITY

We may think we know exactly what we need, or indeed what people we know need. If so, there's a good chance we'll become indignant when God answers in a different way. But we might be wrong! If my son asked me for a flick-knife or a set of knuckle dusters for Christmas, but I give him lego instead, it's because I know better. *Remember: God will not give us things he knows are bad for us, even though we're convinced otherwise.* 'If you then, who are evil, know how to give good gifts to your children, how much more will your Father… give good things to those who ask him' (Matt. 7:11).

5. PRAY WITH OTHERS

There's nothing like a relationship with someone else – a friend or colleague, a husband or wife, a parent – to spur us on to prayer. We need keeping up to the mark. We need others to remind us of all the obvious answers to prayer we've received, when we're getting disillusioned about something we haven't received. *Remember: God has given us brothers and sisters in Christ so we don't have to live the Christian life on our own.* Just recall the first words to the most famous prayer ever: not 'My Father in heaven', but 'Our Father in heaven' (Matt. 6:9, NIV).

6. PRAY WITH A BIBLE

The closer we are to the Bible, the more likely we are to be in tune with God's will when we turn to him in prayer. We'll turn examples of God acting to help his people into prompts to thanking him for what he's done for us. We'll turn promises into prayers asking for those blessings to become our experience. We'll turn information about God himself into 'wow'-prayers – prayers of amazement.

Remember: God's taken the trouble to show us his will so we don't have to fumble around in the dark. Think of the first Christians turning to prayer after trouble with authorities. 'Sovereign Lord, who... through the mouth of our father David, your servant, said by the Holy Spirit, "Why did the Gentiles rage...", grant to your servants to continue to speak your word with all boldness...' (Acts 4:24-29).

7. PRAY WITH DISCIPLINE

We live busy lives, most of us. There are plenty of very immediate calls on our time and our attention. So it's the easiest thing in the world to de-prioritise prayer. We find ourselves 'fitting in' prayer into the 'blank' bits of our day, and leaving it at that. It's good to walk with God in this way, but we'll never grow much in our relationship with God if that's as far as it goes. We need to *plan* to pray. Remember: God has given us models of serious prayer for a reason. 'Very early in the morning, while it was still dark, Jesus got up, left the house and went off to a solitary place, where he prayed' (Mark 1:35, NIV).

8. PRAY WITH A PURPOSE

Are your prayers *all* about you? Not good! Are some of them about others? Better! Are they all really about God? That's best of all. Our motivation in praying must not be seeking the fulfilment of our selfish desires, but an increase in the glory of God. We may get the prayer-answers, but as we do, he gets the glory! *Remember: God's ultimate plan is to see his own glory – and that of his Son Jesus – increase.* Think of Daniel, longing for God to hurry up and end the exile: 'Delay not, for your own sake, O my God, because your city and your people are called by your name' (Dan. 9:19).

God is waiting for his children to come to him. So go to it!

CONCLUSION
You, Me and a BIG GOD

John is the big guy in town. Or rather around the river. As far as anyone can see, he's found a niche market. It's called baptism. It isn't a new concept, but he's believed to hold the sole franchise in this neck of the woods. So when Jesus – one of his former clients, would you believe – is spotted delivering the same service to others, a delegation comes to John to report this flagrant breach of his copyright.

> 'Rabbi, that man who was with you on the other side of the Jordan... well, he is baptising, and everyone is going to him.' (John 3:26, NIV)

What will John do? What level of outrage will he show? How will he protect his monopoly?

He won't. Instead, he simply reminds them that he saw this coming – he'd even said so publicly. He compares

himself to a best man, rejoicing that the groom he attends
is united to his bride. Then he says this:

'He must become greater. I must become less.' (John 3:30, NIV)

If there was ever a fit response to what we've seen of God
during the course of this book, that would be it, surely. In
every part of our lives and our thinking, He must become
greater. I must become less.

But that's easier said than done. After all, you and I have
spent years building up – and then building fortifications
around – that ego of ours. It's not going to fall without
a fight. And any good fight needs a battle-plan.

So where will you go from here? Let me make three
suggestions.

- **Listen**. Listen again to what God says about himself.
  Have another flick through the Bible references in this
  book. Look them up and read them in context. Check
  I haven't made them up! Go and bathe in some of the
  great chapters in the Bible where God's stature is laid
  out. Exodus 15, Job 38-39, Psalm 139, Isaiah 40–42,
  Revelation 1 – among others!

  The world around us has a lot to say. And a lot
  of worldly thinking has got into the churches – even
  church leaders and books! Go back to the Bible. Make
  that your authority and your delight.

- **Pray**. It's one thing to be convinced that God really
  is that 'big'; that he really is working out his sovereign
  plans in minute detail from second to second across
  the cosmos. It's quite another thing to *rejoice* in what
  we learn. But actually both need a work of God's Spirit
  in our hearts and minds. The questions are difficult.

There are objections that spring to mind on every side. They've all been answered by someone; but we need mental energy if we're going to answer them ourselves. And we need new God-oriented hearts if the thought of God becoming greater – even at the expense of ourselves becoming less – is going to bring a smile to our faces.

Can I suggest you don't try to travel this path yourself? If you possibly can, find an older and wiser Christian – one you respect and who has themselves carefully worked through these issues themselves. Pray together – and keep at it. This may be painful and it probably won't be swift.

- **Read and reflect**. This book is written as an 'entry level' primer. Although it is a book all about God's providence – that is, the continuing outworking of God's sovereign will in the world – neither of those words (providence or sovereign) has been used a single time in the whole book (until now). Neither has there been any reference to Open Theism, Arminianism, Deism – or any other -ism! That's because I've wanted us to stay close to the Bible and avoid as far as possible theology-speak.

But if you want to dig deeper and explore further, don't worry – I've got plenty of suggestions! Please have a look at www.big-god.info for suggestions on books and online articles / posts that go deeper into these issues.

He must become greater. I must become less. That's my resolution. I pray it may become yours too. As you face suffering, as you present the gospel to those around you, as you make decisions big and small, and as you pray, may you do so in a way that brings honour and glory to our heavenly father – and acknowledges him in all his unshrunk stature and incomparable majesty.

Iron Sharpens Iron
Leading Bible-oriented small groups that thrive
ORLANDO SAER

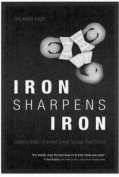

ISBN 978-1-84550-575-2

Iron Sharpens Iron! Small Bible-study groups are great places for Christians both to interact with God's Word and to share their lives with others. They provide relaxed and informal settings which facilitate growth in grace and understanding. Orlando Saer provides a realistic and practical guide for anyone leading or wanting to lead such a group. This book will give you the tools you need as a leader to see your group thrive.

It's the best material I've read on small group Bible study leading and would be useful both for someone leading their first Bible study and for someone who's been leading Bible studies for decades.

9 Marks Blog

Orlando Saer's *Iron Sharpens Iron* may well become the "Bible" for small group studies – as the author's six finely wrought chapters cover virtually everything essential to initiating and maintaining healthy small group Bible studies. There is nothing arm-chair here. No bromides. Saer writes from ground-level, providing us with hard-won advice that is unexceptionably biblical, intensely practical and ever-so-wise. One could wish nothing better for small group ministries than that well-worn copies of this superb book were in the hands of all who aspire to lead. It is terrific, truly the best book of its kind I have read.

R. Kent Hughes
Senior Pastor Emeritus, College Church, Wheaton, Illinois

Five Points
Towards a Deeper Experience of God's Grace
JOHN PIPER

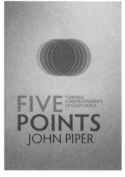

ISBN 978-1-78191-252-2

Grace is the heart of God to do you good when you deserve it least. But do we really know how deeply we don't deserve it? Only God can reveal that to us. He does it through the Bible. And when he does, the wonders of his grace explode with brightness as never before. These Five Points are about how Christians come into being, and how we are kept forever. It reaches back into times past when we were freely chosen. It reaches forward into the future when we will be safe and happy forever. It reaches down into the mysteries of the work of Christ, purchasing the gift of faith for all God's children. And it reaches into the human soul, glimpsing the mysteries of the Spirit's work as he conquers all our rebellion and makes us willing captives of King Jesus.

> I love this new book by John Piper. I don't know of any other brief book on this subject that so manifestly takes us down into the Scriptures and then so wonderfully lifts us up to see the glory of God...
>
> Kevin DeYoung
> Senior Pastor, University Reformed Church, East Lansing, Michigan

John Piper served as pastor of Bethlehem Baptist Church, Minneapolis, Minnesota for thirty-three years. He is the founder and teacher of desiringGod.org, a chancellor of Bethlehem College and Seminary, and has written more than fifty books including *Desiring God* and *Finally Alive*. John and his wife Noël have four sons and one daughter.

Christian Focus Publications

Our mission statement –

STAYING FAITHFUL

In dependence upon God we seek to impact the world through literature faithful to His infallible Word, the Bible. Our aim is to ensure that the Lord Jesus Christ is presented as the only hope to obtain forgiveness of sin, live a useful life and look forward to heaven with Him.

Our Books are published in four imprints:

CHRISTIAN
FOCUS

Popular works including biographies, commentaries, basic doctrine and Christian living.

CHRISTIAN
HERITAGE

Books representing some of the best material from the rich heritage of the church.

MENTOR

Books written at a level suitable for Bible College and seminary students, pastors, and other serious readers. The imprint includes commentaries, doctrinal studies, examination of current issues and church history.

CF4•K

Children's books for quality Bible teaching and for all age groups: Sunday school curriculum, puzzle and activity books; personal and family devotional titles, biographies and inspirational stories – Because you are never too young to know Jesus!

Christian Focus Publications Ltd,
Geanies House, Fearn, Ross-shire,
IV20 1TW, Scotland, United Kingdom.
www.christianfocus.com